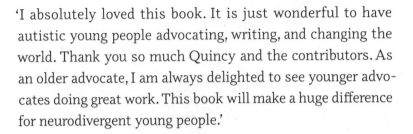

'I absolutely loved this book. It is just wonderful to have autistic young people advocating, writing, and changing the world. Thank you so much Quincy and the contributors. As an older advocate, I am always delighted to see younger advocates doing great work. This book will make a huge difference for neurodivergent young people.'

- Yenn Purkis, autistic advocate and author

'Quincy Hansen's *Shake It Up!* is an essential resource for any autistic teen or young adult seeking to make a positive difference in their community and beyond. In this practical guidebook, Hansen leads aspiring advocates through the steps towards meaningful, effective advocacy, starting with building confidence in one's self-advocacy, right through to the triumphs and pitfalls of platform advocacy. Along the way, Hansen shares many valuable insights from his own experience and the experiences of the eleven diverse young autistic advocates interviewed in the book. We recommend this empowering book to any young autistic person looking to shake things up!'

- Ginny Grant, communications manager, Reframing Autism

SHAKE IT UP!

of related interest

The Spectrum Girl's Survival Guide
How to Grow Up Awesome and Autistic
Siena Castellon
Foreword by Temple Grandin
Illustrated by Rebecca Burgess
ISBN 978 1 78775 183 5
eISBN 978 1 78775 184 2

You Can Change the World!
Everyday Teen Heroes Making a Difference Everywhere
Margaret Rooke
Forewords by Taylor Richardson and Katie Hodgetts @KTclimate
ISBN 978 1 78592 502 3
eISBN 978 1 78450 897 5

The Awesome Autistic Go-To Guide
A Practical Handbook for Autistic Teens and Tweens
Yenn Purkis and Tanya Masterman
Foreword by Emma Goodall
Illustrated by Glynn Masterman
ISBN 978 1 78775 316 7
eISBN 978 1 78775 317 4

The Autism and Neurodiversity Self Advocacy Handbook
Developing the Skills to Determine Your Own Future
Barb Cook and Yenn Purkis
ISBN 978 1 78775 575 8
eISBN 978 1 78775 576 5

SHAKE IT UP!

How to Be Young, Autistic,
and Make an Impact

Quincy Hansen

Jessica Kingsley Publishers
London and Philadelphia

First published in Great Britain in 2022 by Jessica Kingsley Publishers
An imprint of Hodder & Stoughton Ltd
An Hachette Company

1

A CIP catalogue record for this title is available from
the British Library and the Library of Congress

ISBN 978 1 78775 979 4
eISBN 978 1 78775 980 0

Printed and bound in Great Britain by TJ Books Limited

Jessica Kingsley Publishers' policy is to use papers that are
natural, renewable and recyclable products and made from wood
grown in sustainable forests. The logging and manufacturing
processes are expected to conform to the environmental
regulations of the country of origin.

Jessica Kingsley Publishers
Carmelite House
50 Victoria Embankment
London EC4Y 0DZ

www.jkp.com

Contents

Acknowledgments

This book is the fruit of a multi-year labor which could not have been reaped without the help and support of countless family members, friends, and supporters, many of whom have lent me help from across literal oceans. I would like to thank everyone who has in any way supported me during the writing process; I truly could not have done it without you. I would also like to specifically thank the 11 young autistic advocates who agreed to be interviewed for this project: Shadia, Chloe, Clay, Tom, Madi, Jordyn, Siena, Charlie, Alfie, Kat, and Emily. This could never have been completed without you, and it was a pleasure to interact with each of you. In addition, I would like to thank the broader community of autistic advocates who have supported me throughout the years and taught me many of the things that will be written in this book. Ultimately, this was hard; it has sapped my energy, and I could not be more grateful for the support and opportunities provided to me to make this book a reality.

CHAPTER 1

The Journey Begins

*T*here's a specific feeling that may run through your body when you see an injustice in your community, a problem that isn't being addressed, or a circumstance that needs to be changed. A knot ties up in your stomach, your chest tightens as if it were caught in a vice grip, and your head becomes light and airy. Deep within your soul a fire is lit, quenchable only by waters called justice, change, or fairness. Do you recognize these feelings? Do you have a burning passion to take action or to witness change within your own life, your community, or the world? If so, you may have the makings of an advocate.

A popular quote, echoing the words of Mahatma Gandhi, says 'be the change you wish to see in the world.' If one were to sum up what it means to be an advocate in one sentence, this quote would probably do a pretty good job. An advocate is a person who supports, advances, and argues for a specific cause or set of ideas with the purpose of changing the world to be a better place.

An advocate is a dreamer, a thinker, and a visionary. An advocate is someone who sees the world not as it is, but how it could be or should be. An advocate is a person who burns with passion for a particular cause. An advocate is not content to simply sit back and wait for someone else to take action but instead gets up every morning with a mission to make their vision for their community come true. Advocates are those who seek justice for the oppressed and who give voices to the unheard. Advocates are those who rake up the muck that nobody wants to think about and who shine a light on the darkest places within their community in the hope that their light will inspire others to make permanent and positive change.

If the thought of changing the world excites you, then you might just have the makings of an advocate. If there's a particular cause or idea that fills you with drive and a fiery passion, then you're exactly the kind of person needed to make a real difference in the world.

You have probably noticed from the front cover that this is a book about making change as a person who's young and autistic. So, if you're a teen or young adult who identifies as autistic and you desire to make real change in your community, then congratulations! This is the book for you. However, you may be wondering to yourself: what does all this talk about being an advocate and making change have to do with autism? To answer this question, I first need to introduce myself.

My name is Quincy, I'm 19 years old at the time of writing this sentence, and I'm from the beautiful state of Colorado in the USA. Pleasure to meet you! I'm also autistic, and over the past few years I've found that part of my purpose in life is to be an autism advocate, fighting for the acceptance of autism and neurodiversity as well as for the rights of myself and my fellow autistic people. I am the author of the blog *Speaking of Autism...* (the ellipsis is part of the title).[1] I am also a public speaker, consultant, and freelance writer, and I continue to be amazed at the impact that just a few words of mine written online or spoken at a conference can have on people, both autistic and non-autistic alike, from across the world. One day I hope to see a world in which people are more understanding and accepting of autism and other neurological conditions and in which we autistic people feel free to be ourselves without fear of discrimination or prejudice.

My journey as an advocate so far has been like a roller-coaster ride: turbulent at times and agonizingly slow at others, with plenty of ups and downs, unexpected turns, and, I will admit, sometimes quite a bit of screaming. I'm very eager to share with you all the things that I've learned about being an advocate as an autistic young person, and I can't wait to be your guide on your own advocacy journey!

I'm excited because through my work as an autism advocate I have had the opportunity to meet and interact with many fantastic autistic advocates, and I found that many of the traits that make us unique as autistic people also make us some of the world's best change-makers. I truly believe that for a variety of reasons autistic people, including you, have the potential to be, and in many ways already are, some of the most important and note-worthy advocates in the world.

Many of us tend to be very passionate about things that we care about and have a highly attuned sense of empathy, which when combined with an equally relentless sense of

---

1   www.speakingofautism.com

justice and an ability to quickly amass information about a given topic - all of which are often characteristic of autism - can create a sort of 'perfect storm' of traits that make us uniquely suited to advocacy. I have found that many of the other autistic people I have met have some interest in advocacy or social justice even if they don't have a formal platform for advocating. This might describe you as well.

Our community, the autistic community, also has a long history of doing advocacy work, fighting against the discrimination and misinformation that has been directed towards us for decades. As a young autistic person you are inheriting a tradition of advocacy. We are the next generation of great advocates, and even if your topic of advocacy isn't related to autism at all, simply getting your voice out there as an advocate will do wonders for furthering autism acceptance and understanding, in addition to the benefits that come from the advocacy work in your field of choice, of course. What better way to continue this tradition than to leave a legacy of your own?

But beyond simply tradition or the innate talent that many of us possess, I think that it's important for the world to listen to autistic voices, on issues related to autism of course, but in all other areas as well. We are wired to think differently, which provides us with the ability to find solutions to problems that nobody else would be able to see. We are also a minority group, which can give us perspectives on societal issues that others may miss. These factors serve to further elevate the importance of autistic advocates.

And finally, self-advocacy is an incredibly important skill to have as an autistic person, and I think that every autistic person should learn advocacy skills so they can advocate for themselves and their own needs (and, yes, I do believe that every autistic person can be capable of learning how to be a self-advocate, even if that just means being able to say 'no'). Being able to stand up for yourself, your rights, and your needs is a skill that is worthy of developing, and ultimately the tools that are used to advocate for a large-scale cause are not fundamentally different than those that are used to advocate for yourself. Therefore, even if you're not particularly interested in advocating for any particular cause, it is still valuable to learn how to be an advocate for you.

For these reasons, we autistic people can be fantastic advocates. However, this also means we have quite the dilemma: we autistic folk have tremendous potential to change the world, and yet the unique supports and resources we need to be successful as advocates are often lacking. Having a brain that works differently from most other people's comes with its own unique set of strengths and challenges, and while it is certainly true that autism can make us amazing advocates it also means that we may need a little bit more support in some areas or that we may need to do some things a little bit differently. Although every one of us is different, much of the information that is out there regarding how to be an advocate as a young person is irrelevant or difficult to apply for many autistic people because it does not take into account our unique wiring and thinking styles.

This book is an attempt to remedy this situation. It's your very own straightforward, no-nonsense guide to being an advocate and making a real difference as an autistic teen or young adult. Using my personal experiences as a young autistic advocate, in this book I will take you through the steps of finding your voice, setting up your platform for communicating your message, and getting down to business when it comes to making real positive change in your local community, and perhaps even across your country or across the world.

Of course, everybody's situation is different, and no two people have exactly the same skills or access needs. Although this book will be as generalized as possible so that just about anybody can learn something useful from it, chances are that there is something in here that will not apply to you because of the unique ins-and-outs of what makes your life your own. I therefore encourage you to use this book not as a perfect outline for what your own journey will look like, but rather as a guide to inspire you to take action for what you believe in and help you navigate the complex world of advocacy as a young autistic person. If you need to modify the advice or techniques you learn about here to better fit your own situation or access needs, then more power to you to do it. There is no one perfect or right way to be an advocate, so aim to be the best version of yourself rather than trying to compete with someone else.

There are many other young autistic advocates who have embarked on this journey before, so for this book I have also reached out to several of these young change-makers in order to give you some additional advice and perspectives. At the end of each chapter you'll find an interview with one of these teen or young adult autistic activists to give you an opportunity to learn from their experience. At the end of this book we'll also be sitting down and having a conversation with yet more young advocates about their journeys, and we'll use these stories in a set of case studies so that you can gain a better idea of what it's like to be a young autistic advocate. Hopefully you'll find that you relate to one of these champions of change and can use these extra insights while blazing your own trail as an advocate.

I hope that what is written here will inspire you to fight for what you believe in and that it will give you the tools to make a real difference in your community.

The everyday advocate

When many people think of what an advocate is, they picture grand images of giving speeches in front of thousands, writing award-winning books, winning Nobel Prizes, going on months-long hunger strikes, crossing oceans on sailboats, and other grand feats of commitment and international recognition. If this is what you first think of when you think of an advocate, then you might be a little bit skeptical or unsure that you could be an advocate too. After all, it very well might seem like advocates are unusually talented, unusually dedicated people who devote all of their energy and waking life to their cause, and this sort of lifestyle just isn't feasible for everybody.

But what I want you to know is that, in reality, you don't have to live up to this enormous standard to be an effective advocate. Most advocates are just average everyday people with a vision. Sure, you might hear a lot more about famous and even professional advocates who are seeking to make change on a worldwide scale, but most advocates are doing their part to make the world a better place on a smaller but no less important scale. You don't have to give up your entire life to advocacy to make a difference, and as we will see later, you can have an enormous impact even if you reach just a tiny number of people.

So don't be put off advocacy because you're unsure whether you're good enough or talented enough. Once you find your niche and what works for you, your voice can be enough to impact your community. As you progress through your upcoming journey, allow yourself to be what I call an everyday advocate - use the platform you will build and the voice you will develop to focus on getting your ideas out into the world to the best of your ability at every opportunity, no matter how small. Your voice is important, and I really do believe that anybody can be an advocate and that ultimately anybody can change the world, because sometimes even the smallest of actions can make the biggest difference.

So what are you waiting for? Ultimately, the right time to start is now. Let's turn ideas into action! Let's blaze a new trail that will leave a permanent mark on your community. Your advocacy journey begins now, and the only way forward is to dive right in.

Interview 1: Shadia on advocacy and activism

For our first interview, I talked to 20-year-old autism and neurodiversity advocate Shadia Hancock from Victoria, Australia. Shadia is the founder of Autism Actually, an organization that provides presentations, workshops, and other educational resources to teach people about autism. Shadia has several years of experience as a speaker, author, and consultant within the world of autism advocacy, and so I thought they would be the perfect person to give us an introduction to advocacy as an autistic individual.

Here's what Shadia had to say about being an autistic advocate:

What does it mean to you to be an advocate? How would you define advocacy?

For me, being an advocate involves sharing my personal perspectives being autistic. I am passionate about working with teachers, parents, autistic individuals, allied health therapists, and students to answer questions they have about autism and neurodiversity. I feel committed to helping shift the narrative around autism, describing my autism with regard to the neurodiversity paradigm, and using terminology that reflects my positive autistic identity. I also love working with autistic individuals through consultancy and empowering them to foster autistic pride and become advocates for themselves and others. I feel that part of being an advocate is supporting other autistic advocates from a diverse range of backgrounds, including nonspeaking autistics. As a speech pathology student, I try and emphasize that my voice is but one of many and encourage people to listen to many autistic advocates as everyone has unique insights to share.

What drove you to become an advocate? Is there a single moment you can think of where you knew you wanted to help create change?

I discovered my autistic identity at about the age of eight but started reflecting on what being autistic meant for me at around the age of 13. Unfortunately, I started getting bullied and became more conscious about the fact that I am different from others. I was lucky to be introduced to some amazing autistic adults who were actively advocating in the community and saw an autistic adult speak at a high school. They helped me rethink what autism and disability means, from a deficits-based perspective of feeling 'abnormal' and 'disordered', to a neurodiversity-focused lens of being 'differently wired' and 'unique.' I also discovered that being neurodivergent is a natural part of humanity similar to biodiversity. I still remember vividly when my mentors told me that one day I would be an advocate for change like them; at that point, I started to think about how I can share my experiences to help educate others on autism. It started with small actions like telling my teachers when I was overwhelmed, sharing a written piece with staff about my sensory profile, challenges, and strengths, and then eventually presenting to my teachers alongside my mother as part of their staff PD (professional development). My entrepreneurship teacher approached me afterwards and said that I could make a business out of this, and that many community members would benefit from hearing my perspectives. This gave me the idea of becoming an advocate and founding Autism Actually with the support of my teachers and mother.

What has been your favorite or most memorable moment as an advocate?

Traveling to Singapore in 2019 to speak at the Asia Pacific Autism Conference was a huge milestone in my advocacy career. It was surreal being able to travel alongside my mother, my primary support and advocate, as well as my autistic mentor. I was accepted to speak twice, and one session was a full house. It was an incredible experience. It felt like a significant personal accomplishment; the last time I traveled overseas was when I was eight years of age, and whilst it was difficult in some ways due to transitioning and the change in routine, it was powerful to know that I could achieve it with the right support and preparation.

What makes a good advocate? Are there any qualities that you think a good advocate should have? Have you found that autistic people often possess any of these qualities?

I feel that advocacy comes in so many forms that it is difficult to list specific qualities that make a good advocate. For myself, I feel that what has made my advocacy so rewarding is being able to listen to other advocates, learn from them, and share my own perspectives on a variety of issues. I think it is worthwhile being aware of common issues within the autistic and wider community, common misconceptions that may arise, and what you are comfortable discussing in a public forum. I also researched my target audiences such as parents, teachers, and students, and questions that arose frequently during presentations. My values mean I try to come from a place of empathy whilst standing by my own beliefs. This commitment I tend to observe in fellow autistic advocates, and I often learn a lot from them as they have unique perspectives on a variety of issues. I feel it is important to think about what you wish to achieve as an advocate and what forms you are comfortable speaking about. Advocacy can come in many forms, whether it is presenting, consulting, or being active on social media.

Why do you think it's important that autistic young people become advocates?

As a young autistic person my journey of self-acceptance was guided by the perspectives of fellow autistic young people and autistic adults. Do not underestimate the power of autistic voices, regardless of age. Many people would give me feedback that it was powerful hearing from a personal perspective as we know what it feels like to be autistic and how we are perceiving certain things in our environment. This can also be helpful for younger autistic people that may not be at the point where they are comfortable advocating. My mother benefited greatly from reading about autistic individuals and their experiences of issues such as sensory processing, interoception, and emotional regulation. Autism is a diverse spectrum, which means that not every autistic person is the same. I learn a lot from autistic young people, particularly those who may have different experiences to mine. For example, nonspeaking autistic individuals have taught me that speech is not the only valid form of communication.

What advice, if any, would you give to an aspiring young autistic advocate who wants to make change in the world?

As mentioned before, one of the first things I did was identify in what form my advocacy was going to go. At first it was just presentations and consultancy, but then it branched out to social media, blog posts, and YouTube videos. I think it is important to follow your passions and focus on aspects of advocacy you are keen to discuss. I also benefited from engaging with opportunities to learn from experienced advocates on how to expand my knowledge and advocacy efforts. I found these outlets through autistic-led organizations, disability specific organizations, and leadership and entrepreneurship workshops.

Shadia can be found online at the following:
Facebook: Autism Actually[2]
Instagram: @autismactuallyau
On the web: www.autismactually.com.au

---

2   www.facebook.com/autismactuallyau

CHAPTER 2

A Lesson from the Blobfish

Building self-confidence

Off the coast of Australia there lives an animal called the blobfish, known scientifically as *Psychrolutes marcidus*, which in 2013 was voted the 'world's ugliest animal' in an internet poll. The most famous pictures of this fish upon which the dishonor of 'world's ugliest' was given were taken after the fish had been brought up from the bottom of the ocean to sea level on a boat. In these pictures, this fish looks incredibly strange, some would even say disgusting, with slimy pink skin, a droopy bloated face, tiny floppy fins, and a little trail of mucus running out of the corner of its mouth. But the thing is, the blobfish doesn't actually look like this when it's swimming in its natural habitat. In fact, it looks pretty much like a normal fish.

You see, the blobfish lives incredibly deep in the ocean, at depths between 610 and 1220 meters (about 2000 to 4000 feet) below the ocean's surface. Water is very heavy, and so the blobfish is under enormous physical pressure in its natural habitat and is specially adapted for this environment.

However, since most pictures of the animal had been taken at sea level after the fish had undergone rapid decompression from being pulled out of the ocean's depths, these pictures represent a bloated carcass of the fish rather than what it actually looks like while alive.[1] It would be as if you were sucked out of the airlock of a space station without a space suit and someone tried to pass off your desiccated corpse as an accurate representation of what you look like.

People were so quick to call the blobfish ugly that they never stopped to consider that they were looking at an amazing creature that was simply out of its element. Very few recognized the blobfish for what it actually was: an animal with the ability to survive in places where very few other living things can manage. As autistic people we are, in a sense, just like the blobfish being pulled up from the ocean. We live in a world that is not set up to accommodate our needs or adequately support us, and people are quick to point out our struggles or perceived failings.

Autism and autistic people are heavily stigmatized in the world as it currently is, and I don't want to shy away from this fact because the sad truth is that if even if you spent a portion or all of your childhood undiagnosed or misdiagnosed (as frequently happens) you probably picked up on the negative way that people who think differently are perceived and talked about. We are often told that our ways of communicating, regulating, feeling, and moving are wrong. We are often told that we need to pretend to be non-autistic at all

---

1   Shultz, Colin. 'In defense of the blobfish.' *Smithsonian Magazine*. 2013. www.smithsonianmag.com/smart-news/in-defense-of-the-blobfish-why-the-worlds-ugliest-animal-isnt-as-ugly-as-you-think-it-is-6676336

costs, even if it comes at the expense of our own well-being and happiness. And it is in this unideal environment, like a blobfish on the surface, that we are often judged and declared incompetent or broken, with people unable to see how amazing we can be if we are appropriately supported.

Unfortunately, this means that many people like us end up with low self-esteem and a low sense of self-worth. When you grow up being barely supported, misunderstood, and bullied this is bound to happen. I remember facing this culture of autism negativity head on when I was a young teen before I entered high school. I remember hearing from behind closed doors that I would never go on to graduate from school, or obtain my goals, or amount to anything. The actions of teachers told me that my way of simply existing was wrong and disruptive, that I didn't know how to be a good friend, and that if I simply acted more 'normal' and was interested in different things then I wouldn't be bullied so much.

In a 2020 blog article where I wrote about my past experience with school I said:

> Every day felt like a roulette wheel; a random roll of the dice as to whether I'd have a meltdown, or be sent to the office and spend the rest of the day in a little room with nothing but a desk (because I was being 'disruptive'), or be punished for running out of the classroom from being overwhelmed, or be verbally harassed by other students to the point I was uncontrollably sobbing. The principal once called my mom and said she had to pick me up early because she thought I looked too agitated. It's not like

literally every day ended in a major catastrophe, but it was enough that it sure felt that way.

I wanted so badly just to be '*good*'. What I think I knew deep down but couldn't apply or articulate is that I experienced tsunami-sized Big Emotions that I couldn't process or handle, and that my sensory system was constantly overloaded or out of whack. I also simply needed someone, anyone, to believe in me, to treat me as a valuable student with potential rather than just a Problem to be dealt with and sent away as efficiently and conveniently as possible. This model of autism is presented more overtly in some cases than in others, but it is nearly always perceived to some degree by autistic people.[2]

The good news is that, as we will discover, this overwhelming negativity surrounding autism is largely unfounded and irrational. The bad news is that this deficit model is so prevalent in the lives of autistic young people that it's very easy to internalize and believe. This is a severe systemic problem that is rooted in the unfair way that society sees autism and autistic people. However, as an advocate it is very important that you have a strong sense of self-confidence and self-worth, so learning how to overcome negativity about who you are is paramount.

There was a TEDx Talk I saw recently titled 'The Skill

---

2   Hansen, Quincy. 'They Were Wrong.' Speaking of Autism.... 2020. https://speakingofautismcom.wordpress.com/2020/07/22/they-were-wrong

of Self Confidence' where Dr Ivan Joseph of Wilfrid Laurier University defined self-confidence as 'the skill of...having the ability to believe in yourself to accomplish any task, no matter the odds, difficulty, or adversity.'[3] I love this definition of self-confidence because it specifically defines self-confidence as a skill, and because it is a skill this means that with practice it can be improved and built upon. Developing self-confidence is one of the most important first steps on your journey as an advocate because advocacy relies on you becoming the driving force for change. It takes a certain amount of high self-esteem and self-worth to see yourself as what you really are: someone with the capability to make a big impact for good in the world. In this chapter, we will look at ways that you can overcome this deficit model and grow in your own self-confidence.

Neurodiversity

I went through my own period of self-doubt and low self-confidence at a time in my life when I was wrapped up in the negativity that people felt about me because I was not properly understood or supported. One of the biggest things that helped boost my self-confidence was when I learned about and slowly embraced the neurodiversity paradigm. A paradigm is essentially just a way of thinking about something, with the current paradigm surrounding autism revolving

---

3   Joseph, Ivan. 'The Skill of Self Confidence.' YouTube, uploaded by TEDx Talks. 2013. www.youtube.com/watch?v=w-HYZv6HzAs

around negativity and a focus on deficits and conforming to non-autistic standards. The neurodiversity paradigm provides an alternative lens through which we can view autism.

So what is neurodiversity? The word 'neurodiversity' is a combination of the words 'neurological' and 'diversity.' Neurology is the way that a person's brain is wired, which can affect the way we think, move, talk, learn, process sensory information, and so much more. Diversity refers to the differences that exist between people. For example, some people have lighter skin while others have darker skin, some people are taller and some are shorter, and our eyes and hair come in a multitude of colors. Diversity can also take the form of differences in expression of culture and sexual orientation. As humans each of us is unique because we are diverse. Neurodiversity, therefore, is simply the recognition of the diversity that exists in human neurology.

Although nobody's brain works exactly like anybody else's, it is possible to group people into categories called neurotypes based on patterns in their neurology. Most people's brains work similarly to most other people's brains, and so most people can be placed into a category called 'neurotypical' because they have the most common neurology. People who are not neurotypical because our brains work differently than most others are called 'neurodivergent.' As a society, we have further classified neurodiverse people into different named categories, based again on patterns of how our brains work. Autism is one such category, as is ADHD (attention deficit hyperactivity disorder), dyslexia, OCD (obsessive compulsive disorder), dyspraxia, and many others. It is possible to have multiple neurodivergences, and indeed many autistic people can also be described as being neurodiverse in other ways in addition to being autistic.

There is a large amount of diversity in the human population, including neurological diversity. And, biologically speaking, this is a good thing. Populations with high amounts of diversity tend to be healthier and better able to overcome adversity and respond to changing conditions. According to the neurodiversity model, this means that neurodivergences such as autism are important parts of the human condition that are worthy of being celebrated and preserved just as other forms of diversity are worthy of being celebrated and preserved.

By extension, the neurodiversity paradigm would reject the idea that autism is something wrong with a person, or that autism is inherently a deficit that must be corrected at all costs. Rather, it views autism as part of the natural diversity that exists in the human population. It recognizes that while autism comes with its own set of unique challenges and disabilities it also comes with its own set of unique strengths.

As an autistic person, understanding and embracing the neurodiversity paradigm will help to boost your self-confidence because it acts as a counter-narrative to autism negativity. It certainly helped me improve my own sense of self-worth. The neurodiversity paradigm says that autistic people are not simply broken versions of non-autistic people, that autistic people are just as valuable as non-autistic people, and that autistic ways of being are equally as valid as non-autistic ways of being. You don't have to be ashamed of being autistic! It's not a negative characteristic or a flaw.

The neurodiversity paradigm also provides a framework for autism acceptance and even autistic pride simply because it does not view autism through the lens of a deficit-focused model. Many autistic people including myself have chosen to embrace an identity as autistic and recognize autism as an important (and never inherently negative) part of who we are. I would invite you to do the same.

You may notice that throughout this book I am using the identity-first adjective phrase 'autistic person' rather than 'person with autism.' This is intentional and is also rooted in the neurodiversity paradigm. It is intentional because, for one thing, it appears that most autistic people prefer identity-first language, but it is also intentional because it allows me to recognize and embrace autism as an identity. People who advocate for the use of 'person with autism' often do so to try to separate the person from their autism because they view autism through the deficit model and think of autism as an inherently negative attribute. However, the neurodiversity paradigm does not view autism as either inherently negative or inherently positive but as a characteristic that colors who a person is. We use all sorts of identity-first labels to describe ourselves and the ways we are diverse, such as athletic, female, blonde, and so on. Since autism is not a personal failing or negative characteristic, why would we treat it any differently? I would, however, empower you to use and defend whatever words you use to describe yourself.

There is a common myth about the neurodiversity paradigm that needs to be addressed: that it doesn't recognize the difficulties that come with autism or that it doesn't recognize autism as a disability. Neither of these is true. I have no problem admitting the fact that being autistic is certainly not always like sunshine and rainbows on a pleasant walk through the park. Being autistic can be very difficult, and it often presents a lifetime of challenges for us because the world is simply not set up to accommodate autistic people. The neurodiversity paradigm does not claim anything different, but rather takes a more balanced view and sees autism as a natural part of human diversity and recognizes both unique challenges and strengths that come with autism.

The neurodiversity paradigm also does not claim that autism is not a disability, but rather generally takes the position that autism is a disability because society is not set up to adequately support us, not because there is something inherently wrong with autistic people. Therefore, autistic and other neurodiverse people should be supported and accepted rather than 'cured' or changed, so that we can embrace our greatest strengths and talents while staying true to our authentic selves. Similarly, the neurodiversity paradigm is not about only focusing on those who have low support needs or are unusually talented. Neurodiversity is about recognizing and embracing every person, no matter how great their disability may be or how much support they may need, as valuable people who are diverse but not broken, worthy of being supported but not damaged, and understood rather than stigmatized.

Under the neurodiversity paradigm, autism is not presented with a high degree of stigma or as something to be ashamed of, and it is much easier to build self-confidence and a sense of self-worth under this framework than under a model based on negativity. The neurodiversity paradigm will also hopefully help you recognize what supports you need in place and under what conditions and environments you work best so that you can identify your talents and use these as a scaffold to support your own self-confidence.

Finding community

The neurodiversity paradigm can serve as an important lens through which to view your autism in a positive light. However, it is unfortunately still very easy to internalize the negative deficit-centered view of autism that persists in the world. I have noticed that there are many autistic people who agree with and understand the neurodiversity paradigm and yet still find themselves battling low self-esteem because of the prevalence of autism stigma. Paradigms are, by definition, a new idea that changes the conventional way of thinking, and so can be difficult to fully embrace even if they are understood.

One of the things that most helped me to build a positive self-image was seeking out the company of people who are like-minded, specifically other autistic people who embrace the neurodiversity paradigm. I felt very empowered when I saw the writings of autistic people online who were open about being autistic and didn't see autism as a negative thing, many of them going so far as to say they were proud to be autistic! I read as people described going through the exact same things as me and experiencing the world in the exact same way as me, and I had never felt so connected to a group of people before. In all this I came to realize that there was nothing wrong with me, autism is not a flaw in who I am, and that I was absolutely not to blame for the difficulties I was having because my support needs were not being fully met. I learned to accept myself as an autistic person rather than feeling like I was constantly failing at living up to an arbitrary standard that I was not built for, and I had no real desire to reach anyway.

By simply reading and listening to the words of those who already embraced neurodiversity and autism positivity I began to understand and embrace these ideas as well, and within six months I had transitioned from a low point in my life in terms of self-esteem to having the highest level of self-confidence I had ever experienced. By seeking out the virtual company of those that embraced these points of view I learned to accept that 'I am autistic. That is okay. It is part of what makes me who I am, and I do not need to change in order to be worthy of acceptance.' And through this self-confidence came the yearning desire to do my own advocacy and spread this message that improved my life so greatly.

So, I encourage you to do the same. Seek out the voices of people who will reinforce positive messages and ideas in your life. If you can, try to find people who are around your age. When you have engaged with people who share your outlook on life those ideas will be reinforced over time, and slowly you can begin to embrace a positive autistic identity and through that identity begin to build self-confidence and a positive self-image.

Now, I know that a lot of you probably started to feel very anxious when I started to talk about seeking out others. Social anxiety is very real for many people like us because we've probably gone through life experiencing a lot of social rejection, and many of us find it difficult to communicate about certain things. Hopefully I can reduce some of that anxiety by telling you that when I say 'engage' here I don't necessarily mean that you have to directly interact with anybody. Engagement could mean reading through internet forums or blog posts, listening to podcasts, or watching videos. In all these cases you don't have to be actively involved with anybody, but they still count as engagements because ideas are being communicated to you that can help strengthen a positive self-image.

On the internet there exists a thriving community of autistic people who embrace neurodiversity and a positive autistic identity. A good place to start if you're looking for good autistic bloggers and authors to read who are around your age would be the people we interview in this book (check out the interviews at the end of each chapter and the case studies section at the end of the book). The internet also offers lots of excellent opportunities for you to chat with other autistic people via social media or online forums if you desire to do so; however, if you're under the age of 18 you should seek your parents' permission and guidance before engaging with strangers over the internet (for more information on staying safe online, see Chapter 5).

It might also be possible to find an in-person group of autistic teens and/or young adults that meets near you, though I have found that ones that exist outside of any therapy context and are supportive of building a positive and natural autistic identity are rare (and of course you should exercise extreme caution when deciding to attend in-person meet-ups as well). Peer mentoring services for autistic people may exist in your area as well if you're lucky. Believe me when I say that it is a wonderful feeling to find a community of like-minded autistic people who are accepting and understanding of you.

'But Quincy...' you might be thinking to yourself. 'I really want to meet other autistic people my age who might be interested in neurodiversity, but there's nothing around me like that.' Well, perhaps you could be the one to start something like it! There's no reason why you couldn't be the one to start a support group or peer mentoring program for autistic teens or young adults in your community.

Belonging to a community of autistic people who embrace a positive autistic identity can help you to overcome much of the internalized autism stigma that might be preventing you from developing self-confidence and a positive self-image. Such a community can also help you learn more about yourself and support you so that you can become a more successful advocate.

Practicing self-confidence

I'm sure we've all seen highlight reels of professional athletes on TV making superstar plays on the pitch, court, or field. A baseball player hits a huge homerun, a footballer kicks an impossible goal, or a basketball player makes a three-point buzzer-beater shot to win the game. But how do you think that those athletes were able to pull off such amazing plays? The answer is lots of practice and repetition. Athletes spend lots of time practicing the same movements over and over again. In between games basketball players shoot hundreds of free throws, baseball players hit hundreds of balls, footballers dribble around hundreds of cones, and NFL quarterbacks throw hundreds of passes. Musicians practice in this way too, playing the same scale on their instrument over and over to improve their playing technique or practicing their solo many times before they perform it on stage. In any case, practice and repetition are necessary for getting better at a particular skill.

Remember that self-confidence can be defined as a skill, which means that with enough practice and repetition it can be improved. So, what do practice and repetition look like for building self-confidence? Well, since self-confidence is ultimately a mindset built upon your own viewpoint of yourself, practicing positive self-talk to help you embrace a mindset that focuses on your unique strengths and talents can go a long way towards building up your self-esteem.

One way of practicing a self-positive mindset using repetition is through positive self-talk. This means intentionally repeating to yourself things like 'I am valuable,' or 'I am loved,' or even something as specific as 'I know more about cars than most professional mechanics.' Whatever makes you feel good about yourself. Or, if you're like me and don't really think in words, you could visualize yourself enjoying a favorite activity you're good at, hearing a favorite person talk well about you, or remembering a moment in the past when you felt proud and confident. Symbols can be a good way to remember the meaning behind abstract concepts; for example, a rainbow-colored infinity symbol is often used to represent neurodiversity, so you could envision a rainbow infinity sign (or print one out and carry it around with you!) to help you remember your value and completeness as a person with a diverse neurology. Repeat these positive thoughts to yourself over and over again, say them out loud, or even draw them out if you have to. Just like a basketball player shoots hundreds of baskets to practice for the big game, you are practicing viewing yourself through a positive lens, which ultimately makes it easier to build self-confidence.

Oftentimes, I find myself thinking negative thoughts about myself or my abilities. I'm sure this is super common among autistic young people like us, especially if we grew up in an environment in which we were constantly under pressure to meet some goal pressed upon us by others. If you find yourself frequently thinking negatively about yourself or your abilities, one technique that has helped me to practice reversing this is with the word 'yet.' You see, time is always moving forward and nobody is static, so if you find yourself thinking things similar to 'I can't do thing XYZ' simply add the word 'yet' to the end. 'I can't play the C major chord on my guitar…yet.' 'I can't solve this math problem…yet.' 'I can't go to the grocery store by myself…yet.' This reframes your thinking from focusing on what you have trouble with in that moment to a mindset of persistence and self-belief. It helps you stay forward-thinking instead of defining yourself based on your perceived failures.

If we fail to meet an expectation that we have set for ourselves or has been set for us by society or someone else, we may be tempted to think that we must not be trying hard enough, or that we are too lazy or lack motivation. This is rubbish. Of course you're trying as hard as you can, why wouldn't you be?

In these instances, a powerful phrase you can tell yourself is 'I'm doing the best that I can.' Because it's the truth. We, as people, do well when we are able, and by reminding ourselves of this fact we bring to the forefront of our minds that we are ultimately good people with good intentions who, like anybody else, sometimes have trouble doing some things, and this is normal and okay. It's not a personal failing; it's simply a part of who we are as humans, for better or for worse.

Also, never underestimate the power that imagining yourself in a confidence-boosting scenario can have in building a positive self-image of yourself. As silly as it may sound, it's been suggested that simply by imagining yourself doing well you can improve your mental health and boost your self-confidence. Imagining yourself doing something amazing, even if it's complete fantasy, can help you feel more confident in yourself, and in turn ultimately use this confidence to do amazing things in real life. So why not imagine yourself playing on stage at a massive rock concert in front of a huge crowd with your favorite band? Or making a world-changing scientific discovery in a top research lab? Or exhibiting art at a gallery in Paris? Whatever scenario makes you feel strong and confident, don't be afraid to utilize it as an imaginary practice space for holding yourself in high regard and being confident in yourself.

Visualization as a confidence-booster doesn't have to be limited to fantasy either. Whenever I'm about to present at a conference or give a speech I always envision myself giving the presentation or speech in a cinematic style, seeing my bold words move the audience and being met with acclaim. Sometimes this little confidence boost has probably been what's gotten me through the speech. I've given presentations and speeches where I was worried I was going to fall over because my legs were shaking so badly from nervousness. I've given presentations and speeches where, because my speech is often unreliable, I was sure I was going to lose my words and not be able to talk anymore in the middle of the presentation. But each time I've stayed upright and kept my mouth moving in the right way to produce the right words in the right order just as I had practiced, and the audience has loved it.

We'll talk a little bit more about public speaking later on, but my point is that you shouldn't be afraid to use visualization and positive self-talk techniques to give yourself a little boost even if you've already built up high self-esteem. This is a useful skill to have in life in general, but it's even more important for the aspiring advocate.

Finally, though they won't work for everybody, the things I've mentioned in this section have also been useful for me for combating anxiety, and I imagine they could be helpful for others as well. Being autistic means that many of us tend to experience anxiety in waves, with repetitive negative scripts running through our heads. One thing I have found that helps sometimes when I suddenly start feeling super anxious is to try to flood out the anxiety by filling my head with positive self-talk and happy memories to dilute the anxiety. I will repeat good things about myself over and over or try to focus on something positive I have done. While I fully admit this is not even close to a perfect cure for anxiety, it has been something that has helped me a lot in the past.

Finding and embracing your strengths

Think back to when we were talking about the blobfish at the beginning of this chapter. The key lesson to be learned from this squishable swimmer is that ability is dependent on both context and environment. The blobfish is an incredible animal that has the amazing talent of living in the cold, dark, crushing depths of the deep ocean where few other living things can manage to survive. However, this talent went completely unrecognized when the blobfish was pulled out of its habitat and criticized for the appearance of its bloated corpse.

Like the blobfish, I believe that everybody, and that includes you, has talents and strengths that can only be fully realized in the right context and environment. People may unfairly judge us for not performing the same way as everyone else in some contexts, but given the right environment, circumstances, and supports I think that we all can find that we have many unique skills and talents.

Another way of thinking about this concept is through the famous quote often attributed to Albert Einstein that says, 'everyone is a genius, but if you judge a fish by its ability to climb a tree it will spend its whole life feeling as if it were stupid.' This essentially means that comparing someone to an unnatural standard means overlooking the strengths and talents that they have in favor of what they were never suited to do in the first place. You could change the analogy up and imagine being disappointed in a squirrel because it cannot swim like a fish or judging a lizard for not being able to fly like a bird. Just because a lizard cannot fly does not negate its ability to walk up walls, and a fish not being able to climb does not negate its ability to swim through the ocean.

The same goes for people, especially autistic or otherwise neurodiverse people like us. We may not have the same skills in every area as most other people, but this does not negate the amazing skills we do have if we are placed in the right environments and in the right contexts. The key, therefore, is to try to identify what these strengths are and in what environments they can be realized so that we can exploit these strengths in our day-to-day lives and in our advocacy work and build a positive self-image based on them.

Unfortunately, for many of us it can be difficult to find our strengths. I grew up in an environment where much of the focus was placed on all the things I couldn't do, and that made it very difficult for me to realize what I was good at. For a long time I didn't think I was particularly good at anything. In fact, for a while what is perhaps my greatest strength, my ability to write, wasn't something I realized I had because at one point I was testing well below my grade level in writing on standardized tests. It wasn't until I was around 13 or 14 that I began to realize what I was good at. So don't be concerned if you're in a similar position and can't think of what your strengths are. You will figure them out eventually, and your strengths and talents may even lie in an unexpected place.

One of the first useful things you can do to help yourself start finding your strengths is to become your own best supporter. Don't be afraid to take a little bit of credit for the things you've done well. And when I say things you've done well, I mean literally anything. You passed a difficult section in a video game? Awesome, cheer yourself on! You made macaroni and cheese in the kitchen and it tasted super good? You go, that's a victory! I hope you see the point: every little thing you do is worthy of praising yourself, which is an especially important thing to do for yourself if everyone else just wants to focus on what you can't do.

Getting into the habit of congratulating yourself will help boost your self-confidence of course, but it can also help you figure out your strengths by allowing you to recognize patterns in what you are good at. This is also why it's important to congratulate yourself for the little things as much as the big things, because your biggest strengths may not be in obvious areas. Your strengths don't necessarily have to be in academics, or athletics, or in the arts, or in some other special talent in order for them to be valuable. Your strength could be that you're good at a particular type of video game, or that you're a good cook, or that you're good at identifying birds. Your strengths could be a personal thing, like being good at writing jokes, or being creative and always thinking up new solutions to problems, being very generous, being very loyal, or caring for people no matter what.

No matter what you're good at, no matter how mundane, you can use these strengths in some way to spread your message as an advocate. We'll get to how to apply this a little bit later, but for now keep cheering yourself on and looking for those little things that you're good at, because I promise you that you do have your own strengths, even if you haven't found them yet.

As I've mentioned before, in many ways being autistic can give us strengths that most other people may not have.

For example, some of us are incredibly empathetic and are good at connecting with other people's struggles, some of us are fiercely loyal to those we care about, and some of us have the ability to hyperfocus on a task of interest to the point of being intensely productive. Another strength that many of us have as autistic people is our interests, which very often can be incredibly deep and focused. I know that I have a large knowledge base in the areas I'm interested in, such as insects, natural history, and heavy metal music. In the past I've been able to hold my own in highly technical conversations with professional paleontologists and entomologists simply because I have such a large knowledge base in these areas from being so well read. Perhaps you have a similar level of deep knowledge in a subject you're passionate about.

This deep level of knowledge in a subject can itself be considered a strength. Being knowledgeable about a particular subject can help you approach advocacy work from a new angle that many other people would not consider. Here's an example: Let's say that an activist was concerned about the effects of climate change on global biodiversity and was advocating for better species protection measures to be put in place to prevent the total extinction of some of the earth's rarest lifeforms. If this advocate were interested in, say, dinosaurs and fossils, they might use this knowledge in their advocacy work by citing the fossil record to show how species have responded in the past to rapidly changing climates to emphasize the importance of putting protection measures in place. In this example, a deep knowledge in an area of interest was useful for advancing a particular cause. If you have a deep knowledge base in a particular interest this specialized knowledge could come in handy when advancing your cause, even in ways that you may not recognize at the moment.

Specialized passionate interests can also act as a major strength in advocacy work because they may give you opportunities to connect with many people in your community whom you are trying to reach with your message. Additionally, as you pursue your passions you may find other talents that you didn't even know you had. My advice to you therefore is to embrace all your interests, no matter what other people tell you.

Unfortunately, our interests as autistic people are often over-pathologized or downplayed, and we are sometimes told that we shouldn't be so interested in the things we're passionate about. Sometimes we're told that our interests are 'cringey' or not 'age appropriate' or that it's socially unacceptable to be so deeply interested in one particular subject. I remember being told by a school counselor that more people would like me if I would stop talking about insects so much.

Don't listen to any such nonsense. There is no universal law that says you can only be mildly interested in a predetermined list of subjects. It is perfectly fine for you to be passionate about whatever it is you are interested in. Please believe me when I say that it is perfectly fine for you to keep learning more about what you're interested in. It's perfectly fine to talk all you want about whatever you're interested in. Don't let anyone tell you otherwise. Because if you're afraid to fully embrace your interests, not only are you letting others rob you of personal joy, you are also not taking advantage of an opportunity to find and explore your strengths.

Embracing yourself

The final and perhaps most significant stage in building self-confidence and a positive self-image is to begin to truly embrace your authentic self. Embracing yourself means being comfortable with and proud of who you are as a person. It means not feeling like you have to hide any parts of your identity from the world. It means being able to say proudly, 'I am who I am, and who I am is okay.' This doesn't mean giving up on self-improvement, but rather means accepting and embracing who you are as a person: your personality, your likes and dislikes, your sense of style, your beliefs, your identities, and other aspects of you that make you, well, you. Fully embracing yourself is a process and a journey, and it involves putting into practice everything we've talked about in this chapter so far: embracing your neurological makeup via the neurodiversity paradigm, finding a community of like-minded people to reinforce autism positivity, practicing positive self-talk, and finding your strengths. Each of these strategies will help you to begin down the path of self-acceptance.

It's not a short journey; in fact it's probably a lifelong one. I continue to struggle to fully embrace myself to this day. Like many autistic people I struggle with intrusive thoughts, and I often compulsively wonder if I'm a good person, or if I do the right things, or if I'm too much of a burden on the world. You'll also probably struggle with the same as you work more and more towards embracing your authentic self. But as you progress through this journey you will inevitably become progressively more and more self-accepting and confident in your identities, which in turn will make you a better advocate.

Autism inevitably colors much of who we are as people. I would argue this is neither inherently good nor inherently bad. It just is. But the fact that our neurological makeup has widespread effects on who we are means that it is worthy of being embraced and celebrated along with everything else that shapes who we are. Unfortunately, this is a very difficult thing for many of us to do because of the way that broader society views autism and autistic expression.

It is common for many autistic people to be told when growing up that we must adjust the way we live in order not to deviate from what is considered typical. We're told we must speak in the right way, use a specific set of body language, be interested in the right things. We're told that we must stop stimming and stop reacting to painful sensory stimuli. All in all, we are sent the message that our authentic way of living is wrong. We are told, either implicitly or explicitly, that we must construct a sort of 'costume' or 'mask' to hide our autistic-ness at our own expense so that we are indistinguishable from non-autistic people. This entire line of thought is pretty ironic given the current push in schools worldwide to tell students to 'be yourself,' but unfortunately this is a very relatable experience for many, perhaps most, autistic people.

Trying to construct a mask to hide your autism isn't only taxing from a mental health point of view, it also runs counter to embracing your authentic self. Truly accepting yourself means not feeling like you have to change to fit anyone's expectations other than your own. However, after living almost your entire life pretending to be someone you're not it can be difficult to take the mask off. I'd like to offer a little bit of personal encouragement and tell you that it if something makes you happy or comfortable and does not hurt other people it is perfectly alright to engage in it.

It's okay to do 'autistic things' if they make you happier. It's okay to be interested in subjects that are unconventional or others consider immature. It's okay if you need to socialize at your own pace rather than everyone else's. It's okay if you need to pace, or rock back and forth, or chew on things, or flap your hands in order to regulate your senses and emotions or help you think. In short, it's okay to be a little bit 'weird' if it makes you happier and more comfortable. It's okay to be autistic, no matter what all the ignorant people who are trying to use 'autistic' as a playground slur would tell you.

Fully embracing yourself, which includes embracing your needs and necessary supports, also means having the willingness to put your needs and comfort first. This doesn't mean being inconsiderate or unkind to others, and it doesn't mean being self-centered. Rather, it means being willing to stand up for your own comfort and needs even in situations where there may be pressure to conform to a specific standard.

For example, if you're interested in a particular show but one of your peers tells you that it's too childish and you need to 'grow up,' fully embracing yourself might mean disregarding these comments because you know that this show makes you happy. As another example, you might wear and chew on a silicone necklace because it calms you down even though some of your peers or family members tell you it's 'weird.' Being able to stand up for your individual needs as a person can be incredibly empowering and can be a major boost to self-confidence, and it is a sign that you are embracing and accepting who you are as a person.

Concluding thoughts

Building self-confidence and a positive self-image is a journey, and a long one at that. But by remembering the story of our friend the blobfish and applying some of the strategies we discussed in this chapter, hopefully you will have started down the right path. It isn't always an easy thing to do, but being able to develop enough self-confidence that you can put faith in yourself is a very important first step if you wish to be an activist in your community.

In the next chapter, we'll take a look at starting out small as you embark on your journey as an aspiring advocate and discuss choosing your topic, building an advocacy platform, setting goals, and the importance of self-advocacy.

Interview 2:
Chloe on neurodiversity and self-confidence

Being self-confident and building a positive self-image is perhaps the most important first step you can take as an aspiring advocate, in addition to being an important foundation on which to build your personal identity. To get new insights into this important topic, I reached out to 13-year-old autistic advocate Chloe from the United Kingdom. Chloe runs the YouTube channel Chloe Me Just Me, where she creates vlogs about a variety of topics including her life as a PDA (pathological demand avoidance) and autistic teen, and as an advocate is focused on promoting teen mental health, authenticity, positivity, self-care, and positive autistic identity.

You started making videos and advocating for mental health and neurodiversity at a fairly young age. What got you interested in making videos? What got you interested in advocacy?

I started making videos and social media posts because I wanted to be a positive role model and inspiration to others and to share some of my views with the world. When I was younger there were little to no young creators sharing their viewpoints on topics such as PDA, autism, and anxiety, and also neurodiversity. I therefore decided that I wanted to help raise awareness and also stay authentically me in the process. My parents helped me set it up and supported my decision and Chloe Me Just Me started.

What does neurodiversity mean to you? How has having a neuro-diversity mindset impacted your self-image, if at all?

Neurodiversity to me means that it's okay to think differently and learn differently. I see it as more of an ability and a strength. Having a positive mindset and understanding about being a neurodivergent individual has given me confidence to speak and act like myself rather than hiding who I really am. I am not ashamed of my autistic identity, and I am rather proud of all aspects that make me, me!

Sometimes it seems like the world is overwhelmingly negative, especially towards autism and autistic people. What has helped you stay positive and happy about yourself?

I don't let negative perceptions of how people think autism is affect me. They clearly are not educated or well informed on the matter. Living and being autistic gives you so much more understanding and self-awareness. I never let people who have a lacking in knowledge/intelligence impact my self-esteem. If they don't have a clear understanding then why should I allow them to diminish who I am?

In the past, how have you used your interests and talents to build self-confidence?

First off, I have a very supportive family and I really wouldn't be where I am now without them. They have supported a lot of my interests and reassured and facilitated my strengths and my hobbies. By being able to pursue my interests such as YouTube, art, and baking it has boosted my confidence and given me a lot of joy!

What does it mean for someone to be authentic? Why is it important for teens to be authentic?

Being authentic is being true to myself, letting my personality show, and not letting anyone stop that. I am me forever! You will always see all of me: my emotions, quirks, and faults! It's important for teens to be themselves or at least have the opportunity to discover themselves so they are not held back and can have a positive future with a healthy mindset about themselves and good boundaries where they don't allow negative opinions of others get them down.

What advice, if any, would you give to an aspiring young autistic advocate who wants to make change in the world?

My advice to anyone is to just get out there, show yourself, share your experiences, visions, and thoughts. Be confident being you! Just give it a go, there is nothing to lose. People don't change the world by holding back. Be happy being you.

Chloe can be found online at the following:
Facebook: Me Just Me[4]
Instagram: @chloemejustme
YouTube: Chloemejustme[5]

---

4   www.facebook.com/chloemejustme
5   www.youtube.com/chloemejustme

CHAPTER 3

Starting Small

I remember the moment that I decided I wanted to be an autism advocate. It was the spring semester of my first year of high school in 2017, when I was 15 years old. That particular semester I had a period after lunch when I had no classes, and I would often spend the time I had off reading on the internet. This was a time in my life where I was experiencing a dramatic turnaround, as I had recently come out of a very dark place in a toxic school environment and was slowly rebuilding my self-confidence.

I was also starting to explore what it actually meant to be autistic, so naturally I spent a lot of time reading blogs and articles written by other autistic people. In doing so I related very strongly to the way that other autistic people were describing their struggles with school and life in general. I realized that many of the difficulties I and many other autistic people faced came not from anything inherently wrong with us, but rather because most places are not adequately set up to accommodate the needs of autistic people, in addition to the fact there are a lot of misconceptions about autism out there in the world.

This realization, along with my growing desire to become connected with the thriving online autistic community, led me to decide that I was going to become an autism advocate just like all the advocates whose blogs I had been reading. I wanted to add my voice to the pool of autistic people advocating for neurodiversity, autism acceptance, and disability rights so that perhaps one day autistic people wouldn't have to go through the trauma I went through in elementary and middle school.

I had made up my mind that I wanted to be an advocate, and many months of reading had helped me develop enough self-confidence that I could do it. But where to start? At this point you might be in the same position I was in. You're passionate enough about making change that you've decided you want to be an advocate, and hopefully some of the strategies we talked about in the last chapter can help you gain the necessary confidence to do so. But you're probably wondering 'Where do I start?' 'How am I supposed to become an advocate?' 'How will I ever compare to other advocates who seem to have the world as their stage?'

In this chapter we'll answer these questions and talk about launching your very own advocacy platform, starting on a small scale and working up from there as possible or necessary. We'll talk about finding a topic you're passionate about, how to begin to build a platform, setting goals, finding your niche, overcoming executive dysfunctioning to get started, and self-advocacy.

A matter of scale

Recently, the young, autistic climate change advocate Greta Thunberg made headlines worldwide, quickly raising a global platform and gaining the audience of world leaders and the United Nations. Greta is one of many young autistic advocates out there who are making worldwide changes via huge platforms. I know that for me it has often been incredibly overwhelming seeing all of the major accomplishments of young advocates, many of them autistic like myself, and feeling like I have to somehow live up to their level of recognition and involvement. It's very easy to associate advocacy with writing best-selling, influential books, having conferences with world leaders, and giving a dozen TED Talks on an issue that threatens the very existence of humanity. This association has in the past given me anxiety over my ability to ever reach this level of influence, have all the talents necessary to grow my platform, or be able to juggle all the necessary connections to be an influencer on a global scale.

It's overwhelming feeling like you have to live up to this standard to be a proper advocate. But I'll let you in on a little secret: you don't have to be Greta Thunberg, Malala Yousafzai, or Amanda Gorman to be an effective advocate. In fact, the greatest changes in the world don't come from internationally known advocates whose speeches get aired on live TV. The greatest changes come from the collaborative effort of lots of equally as driven yet smaller-scale, focused advocates who set out to focus on making a difference in their own community.

In general, people are far more likely to listen to advocates who belong to their own community or social circle, which means that as an advocate the most potential for making change you have will be with people you already know, or those who are geographically close to you. This doesn't mean that you can't ever aim to expand your reach and make a difference on a broader scale. It simply means that your greatest opportunity to make change in the world will be within your local circles.

The good news is that even small-scale advocacy work can still make a big difference. I've heard that it's been calculated that every single living person on the planet is linked together by seven connections or less. It works like this: one of your friends or anybody else you know likely knows somebody that you don't know. You are one connection away from this person that you don't know, through your friend. In turn, that stranger knows someone else that neither your friend nor you know, and that person is two connections away from you, through your friend and through the stranger that your friend knows. Following this pattern, you are fewer than seven (and for most people, significantly fewer) connections away from every living person on earth, from every member of the British Royal Family, to the President of the United States, to your favorite musician, to the stranger who walked past you in the store.

Your influence as an advocate can therefore grow quickly even if you are advocating only on a very small scale. If you influence someone in your community into thinking differently about something or changing the way they do something this influence can spread to many people through everyone's interconnectedness, even if you are not personally connected to this change.

And of course, making only small changes in your communities, whether that be in your household, in your school, or in your neighborhood, is a worthy goal by itself and will play a huge role in making the world a better place. Not to mention that the smallest form of advocacy, advocating for yourself to those who you interact with, is one of the most important lifelong skills that you can have as an autistic person.

What is a platform?

One thing that we will be talking a lot about from this point forward is your platform. 'But what's a platform?' you might ask. Well, let me tell you.

In the olden days before the internet, social media, or even a widespread newspaper, when people wanted to get a message across to as many people as possible they'd go to a busy street corner and stand on a stage or platform and start shouting out their ideas. Actually, go to any major city today and you'll probably find people still doing the same thing. People will stand up on a platform in order to amplify their voice, get more attention, and spread their message to more people. Thus, in advocacy your platform is the collection of tools that you use to amplify your voice as an advocate and further spread your message.

Thankfully, nowadays your advocacy platform can be much more than a literal platform. Your advocacy platform could consist of multiple different forms of media, such as social media pages, writing (in the form of blog posts, articles, print publications, etc.), websites, public-speaking engagements, presentations and workshops, videos, and even artwork, just to name a few examples. When building your platform, it's important to incorporate elements that you enjoy and that appeal to your strengths.

In the next chapter we'll talk about many different methods of communicating your message. There are lots of different ways of promoting your ideas and amplifying your message, and with a little creativity you're sure to find some good ways to build your platform.

Choosing your topic

If you've picked up this book and read this far, I hope that you've had enough time to think about what sort of change you'd like to see in your community. Maybe you knew what you wanted to advocate for before you even picked up this book, or maybe you have already gotten started and just need to know what to do next. If that's the case, then great, you're already halfway there! Simply making the conscious decision that you want to make change in the world for the better and understanding what topic you want to advocate for is the first major step in your journey as an advocate. Once you're committed and know your topic you have, to use a metaphor, found the trailhead, and now you can start heading down the path.

Of course, you might not know quite yet what topic you want to focus on as an advocate, or maybe you have lots of different ideas about how you could make a difference. Whatever your situation, any advocacy topic that you will pursue or have already decided to pursue should fall within a certain set of guidelines.

An advocacy topic should:

- be something you are passionate about
- be applicable on a small scale
- feature tangible, concrete goals.

Let's talk about each of these points individually so that you can better shape your topic to maximize potential for change. If you are interested in becoming an activist and advocate but don't yet know what topic or topics to focus on, these guidelines will also help you decide which ideas to advance and what changes you want to make in your community.

CHOOSE A TOPIC YOU ARE PASSIONATE ABOUT

This is perhaps the most important criterion for choosing a field of advocacy. You must be passionate about the topic you are engaging with and must yearn with a burning passion to see the changes you are advocating for. Passion can act as a powerful engine to drive your work as an advocate and can provide the motivation necessary to continue your work even as times get tough. The most effective young advocates in recent times, such as the aforementioned Greta Thunberg, are often characterized by their passion for their topic. They truly desire to see the changes they are advocating for, and they truly believe in the ideas they are advancing.

Luckily, many of us autistic people have a talent for being deeply passionate, deeply interested, and deeply invested in one or more particular topics. Ideally you already know exactly what you want to advocate for (it may be why you picked up this book!) because you're already interested in and passionate about that topic! If you're looking for a cause to get passionate about, a topic of advocacy that comes naturally to many autistic people for obvious reasons is autism and neurodiversity advocacy. A good portion of the autistic advocates we'll be interviewing in this book (as well as me, the author) are autism advocates, though don't feel that just because you're autistic you have to be an autism advocate if that's not what you're interested in. Advocate for the changes you desire to see and follow your passions!

CHOOSE A TOPIC THAT IS APPLICABLE ON A SMALL SCALE

Nearly everyone has dreams of changing the world, and by all means have these dreams because in many ways the world needs to change and there's no reason you couldn't be the one to do it! However, just as a journey of 1000 miles begins with a single step, your advocacy platform should generally start off by reaching those within the smaller social circles that you belong to, such as your family, your school, or your neighborhood. When I first started blogging, my initial intention was to write as a way to communicate with my family and my teachers about autism and how to better support me. Eventually, when I gained enough confidence to do so, I started making my posts public and sharing my writing with people outside of my immediate family, friends, and teachers.

Seemingly overnight my writing had blown up on the internet and I was getting thousands of views from people all over the world! But ultimately, I started with the smallest applicable audience for my message: my own family.

You should also aim to start spreading your message on a smaller scale, not because you're incapable of doing large-scale advocacy or because your message is not good enough for a larger scale, but because starting small will give your platform an opportunity to grow organically and become more refined, while also giving you an opportunity to grow in your advocacy skills. Luckily, just about every advocacy topic under the sun can be applied within your family or local community. Here are some examples:

- Want to fight world hunger? Why not start by raising awareness for food insecurity and hunger in your own neighborhood or city. Start a canned food drive at your school or university or ask for donations to a food bank from friends and neighbors.
- Want to promote autism acceptance and neurodiversity? Maybe you could create and hang up informational posters on autism and neurodiversity at your school or university. You might also try organizing a neurodiversity or autistic pride club at your school or university.
- Want to promote wildlife conservation? Try starting with your own city by writing to your local government on the importance of conserving open space within the city limits for wildlife habitat, or creating a website about the importance of wildlife conservation in your city.

These are just a few examples of how you can start an advocacy platform with worldwide applicability on a small scale. From a small, manageable start your message can quickly grow in size and reach. Think of it like a snowball rolling down a hill. It may start small, but as it picks up speed and continues rolling it grows larger and larger as it picks up more snow. You just have to get the snowball rolling, and a small snowball is much easier to push down a hill than trying to start with a huge snow boulder.

CHOOSE A TOPIC FOR WHICH YOU CAN SET TANGIBLE GOALS

Once you have an idea of what your platform is going to look like (keep reading to the next chapter for some ideas if you're stuck!), the next important step to take is to set concrete, tangible goals for your platform. Goals are useful in giving your advocacy work direction, so that you aren't simply 'wandering into the dark.' Goals are the markers that will define your path as an advocate. Whichever path you take is up to you, but setting goals for yourself is a way to plan what route to take.

Obviously, the goal of any advocate is to make a positive impact on their community. This is the broad, overarching goal of all forms of advocacy. But when I'm talking about goal setting here, I'm not talking about your overarching goals; I'm talking specifically about practical goals relating to your platform and your work as an advocate - goals about the physical things you are going to do to attempt to advance your message more than goals about the outcomes of your advocacy. This type of goal would look something like 'by the end of the year

I will have written ten blog posts for my website' rather than 'by the end of the year at least 100 people will agree that they need to take action with me.'

The intent of this type of goal setting is not to make you stressed about reaching some milestone or anxious when you don't reach a specific goal. Don't worry too much about trying to force yourself out of your comfort zone because you're pushing yourself too far to reach some goal! The intent of this type of goal setting is purely to provide you with a roadmap of sorts to help you know what to start working on next, especially early on as an advocate before many opportunities are presented to you on their own. If you ever get to a point where you feel stuck with your advocacy work, you can use your practical goals to figure out what's next.

Practical goals can also provide a certain amount of motivation and lower the chances that you'll end up dropping your platform entirely before it ever has a chance to get going. It's sort of like an RPG video game that gives you a list of quests to complete. There's something satisfying about completing quests and checking them off your list, which keeps you progressing through the game. Setting small, manageable goals for yourself can keep you pushing forward via the same psychological trick that these video games use. Keeping a running list of goals like a quest list in a game can also make advocacy work feel more fun!

When setting these types of practical goals, there are a few guidelines that should be followed for them to be productive as 'road markers' of sorts for your path as advocate. To start, goals that you set in this context should be objective and measurable. Generalized goals that are not objective and measurable are not useful for acting as a guide simply because they are too vague and often physically not achievable.

A specific goal would look something like 'I will reach out to my teacher about putting up posters in the classroom to promote awareness of my advocacy topic,' which is different from a vague goal that would read something like 'I will help my classmates understand the importance of my topic.' The first goal is measurable in that it has a specific condition for being met (meeting with the teacher) and mentions a specific action. The second goal is too vague to be useful because it never specifies an action to take, and it does not have measurable objective conditions under which it can be met. Don't get me wrong, it's not a bad general goal to have; it's simply too vague to inform your practical actions as an advocate.

Second, your specific goals should be within your control. As the purpose of these goals is to provide you with a better sense of what direction to take when building your platform, it's important that these goals can be reached without necessarily relying entirely on the actions of other people. 'By the end of the year I will have written ten blog posts' is a good specific goal to have, while 'by the end of the year my blog will have accumulated 25,000 views' is not because it relies on other people deciding to click to your site, and as such is not entirely in your control. You can focus your energy on writing blog posts, but you can't force a bunch of people to come to your site. While it can be fun to track statistics in a light-hearted manner, worrying too much about goals that are out of your control can lead to much stress and anxiety while not being very beneficial in tracking your personal progress as an advocate.

Finally, it is often recommended that the goals you set for yourself should be time-bound, meaning they should have a self-imposed time limit. However, very often goals that are on a specific time limit can be very stressful to the point that these sorts of goals can be more of a detriment to your progress than actually motivating. Thus, so long as you are self-motivated enough to continue pursuing advocacy work, I don't think you necessarily need to keep to strict timelines for these types of goals if it will cause you anxiety. That said, for many people specific deadlines can be motivating and can even help them overcome struggles with executive functioning, so knowing yourself and how you respond to deadlines is important in determining whether or not you want to hold yourself to a timeline when it comes to goals for your advocacy platform.

No matter what your goals for your advocacy platform are, write them down. You don't have to actually get a pencil or pen and a piece of paper and write if you don't want to; you could also type them into a Word document on a computer, type them into your phone, voice record them, or ask somebody to write them down for you as you dictate. But have some sort of physical copy of your goals somewhere so that you can reference them whenever you get stuck. Whenever you're not sure where to go next you can always check back at your most recent goals for a little bit of self-guidance.

When you have your list of goals written out, take a look at each one, and ask yourself the following questions:

- Is this goal specific?
- Is this goal objective and measurable?

- Is this goal within my control?

If you answered 'yes' to all of these questions, then congratulations, you've written an excellent goal for use in building your advocacy platform! Remember that the purpose of this set of goals isn't to stress you out. It's to act as a guide, sort of like the quests in a video game, and also to help you plan for and envision how your platform will grow in the future. The goals you set will be your trail markers as you grow your platform, and being able to set them is an important skill for being able to keep yourself motivated, on track, and self-determined.

What's in a name?

Once you have figured out what exactly it is you are going to be advocating for, it's important to start thinking about giving your advocacy platform a name. Naming your platform is of importance because later on it will be useful for the purposes of branding and promoting your message. When you can unify all of your endeavors as an advocate under the same name you can more easily grow and unify an audience.

You don't have to decide on a name for your advocacy platform right now, so don't worry if you can't think of anything at this moment. But do start thinking about what you might want a name for your platform to be, because in the next chapter we'll be talking about ways to promote your message, and it's very helpful to have a name for your platform when you set up a website, blog, or social media accounts.

You could try naming your platform after your topic of advocacy, your method of communicating your message, or even just naming your platform after yourself. Another good naming strategy is to base it on a common phrase or slogan; for example, the name of my advocacy platform is 'Speaking of Autism...' (with the ellipsis, it's part of the name) and it is based on the common interjection of 'speaking of which...' It references the fact that autism is an important part of my life due to how it colors the way that I see the world. Wordplay, alliteration, and double meanings could also work well in the title of your platform.

Finding your niche

In ecology there's a principle called niche partitioning, which says that each species fills a particular role in its ecosystem, called a niche, in a way that tends to reduce competition with other species. Think of a forest. In a forest you have all sorts of animals fulfilling different roles: there are squirrels that live in trees and eat nuts, there are birds that fly through the canopy and eat seeds, there are foxes that scamper around hunting smaller animals, and there are bears that eat berries and occasionally other larger animals. Every species has a specific strategy for exploiting its ecosystem's resources so that it competes less with other species and can be more successful within its role.

As an advocate, one of the goals of your platform should be to fill a specific niche within your topic of choice. Chances are you aren't the only person in the world who's advocating for your topic of choice, and so as an advocate in the same area you will be 'competing' against them for influence. Now, it's kind of odd to be described as competing against somebody who has the same goals as you do. After all, you're on the same team and want the same things, so you may be wondering why you should try to compete with them.

In this context though, 'competition' doesn't mean you're trying to get every advocate other than yourself to fail or that you're trying to monopolize the advocacy game in your specific field. It simply means that there are a limited number of people out there who can be reached by any one specific form of advocacy, and so trying to draw from the same pool of people as someone else inevitably means that neither advocate will be able to reach everybody in that pool with their platform, and more often than not it's going to be the established advocate drawing the majority of attention, leaving new advocates such as yourself without an audience.

You should want your fellow advocates to succeed, and you should do your best to encourage them, collaborate with them, and network with them. But if your advocacy platform is filling the exact same niche as someone else's, you're not helping either yourself or the other advocate because you're directly competing with each other instead of maximizing the number of people you both can reach by appealing to slightly different audiences.

If it helps, don't think of yourself as competing with other advocates, think of yourself as attempting to maximize the impact of your advocacy by designing your platform so that it appeals to an unreached audience and so the total influence of your movement grows. Regardless of which way you look at it, you should try to design your advocacy platform in such a way that it fills an empty niche. Having other advocates to look up to as role models is a great thing and can teach you a lot about advocacy, but you should never try to copy the exact form, style, angle, and medium of another advocate.

This doesn't mean that you can't use the platforms of other advocates as a guide to your own or draw inspiration from role models. But you should always try to add your own 'spin' to your platform so that you are not directly competing with another advocate.

Some people will be more easily reached by some methods than by others, and so distinguishing your platform from the rest can help you to reach people that other advocates may not, and in turn increase the influence of your movement and inspire even more real change in the world. To build your own niche within your movement, you might try to:

- change up your communication medium
- change up your angle
- change up your intended audience.

Let's explore each of these options:

CHANGE UP YOUR COMMUNICATION MEDIUM

The next chapter will be devoted entirely to the many different ways that you can communicate your message and tools you can use to support your advocacy platform. As you will see, there are many different media you can use to get your message out into the world and focusing on a unique medium that you enjoy can be a great way to distinguish your platform from that of other advocates. For example, if most of the other advocates in your movement seem to be bloggers, why not try making videos or drawing cartoons to spread your message?

CHANGE UP YOUR ANGLE

Your angle is essentially the unique focus that you have on the issue you are advocating for. It is likely that the field you are advocating in is very complex, so there are probably issues you can bring attention to that not many other advocates have focused on. You can focus on this specific facet of your topic to distinguish your platform from others. Your unique angle can be as simple as your own personal experience. For example, many nonspeaking autistic people who are advocates choose to focus specifically on issues that involve nonspeakers, as this is their primary area of expertise gained through life experience. The angle or focus of these advocates is specifically on nonspeaking autistic people, a subset of broader autism advocacy. Your platform might similarly try to focus on a specific issue or category that falls within your topic of advocacy.

CHANGE UP YOUR INTENDED AUDIENCE

Every advocacy platform will have a specific demographic, or a specific category or categories of people, that it most effectively reaches. Which demographics your platform appeals to depends largely on how and where you communicate your message, the angle you take on your topic, and other advocacy strategies you decide to use. For example, if you're trying to reach people your own age then social media platforms are a great medium for advocacy, but if you're trying to reach people who are older then you may have less luck on something like Instagram than you would from an email list.

It's a good idea to know in advance what demographic is your target when designing your advocacy platform. Are you trying to reach people your own age? Older than you? Perhaps even younger than you? Are you trying to reach people of a specific gender or other identity status? Your target demographic doesn't have to be the only people you are reaching with your advocacy of course, but you will find that, even if unintentionally, your platform will appeal mostly to a particular set of demographics.

The reason I bring this up now is because one of the easiest ways to set your advocacy platform apart from others is to target a demographic that few other people are trying to reach with your topic of advocacy. In fact, if you follow my previous advice and begin by focusing your advocacy on a smaller scale with your local communities, then you're already targeting a unique demographic.

Ultimately, both yourself and your fellow advocates will be more successful if you aim to fill your own niche rather than try to break into someone else's. It's alright to model your own platform based on an advocate you admire, but you also must make your platform your own to ensure you are not directly competing with other advocates. However, this goal can be accomplished with only minor tweaks to your platform.

'Just do it!'

There was a video that went viral a few years ago in which the actor Shia Labeouf was filmed giving an awkward inspirational speech in front of a blank green screen. In the video, Shia screams phrases like 'What are you waiting for? Just do it!' and 'Yesterday you said tomorrow, so just do it!' into the camera, telling the viewer that in order to 'make your dreams come true' you must take the initiative to get started working towards whatever your goals are.[1] But as abrupt and somewhat comedic as the video is, Shia's advice actually isn't all that bad. Very often the biggest thing that prevents people from fulfilling their biggest plans and aspirations is their own inaction. In a sense, we can become our own biggest obstacles.

As an aspiring advocate, you've probably already thought about what your advocacy platform will look like. Maybe you're thinking about starting a blog or website, making posters to hang up around town or around your school, or reaching out to leaders in your community about issues you are passionate about. These are all tasks that can certainly be accomplished; many people like you have done these things and more before. However, the biggest battle you may face in launching your advocacy platform is simply taking the initiative to actually start. Having trouble with this isn't a personal failing and it's nothing that you should feel ashamed of, in fact most people struggle with this, but it does nonetheless

---

1   LaBeouf, Shia. 'Just Do It.' YouTube, uploaded by MotivaShian. 2015. www.youtube.com/watch?v=ZXsQAXx_a00

present a major obstacle in the way of launching an advocacy platform.

To explain why it can sometimes be difficult to start your platform, let's talk a little bit about inertia. In physics, inertia is the idea that an object in motion stays in motion and an object at rest stays at rest (unless acted upon by an external force). If you were to throw a ball in an infinitely large perfect vacuum with no gravity the ball would continue moving in that same direction at that same speed forever. Similarly, a stationary object will never start moving on its own unless it is acted upon by an outside force. You can think of your hypothetical platform, whatever form that may take, as an object at rest. In order to launch your platform you have to overcome its inertia to get it to start moving.

A lot of us autistic people have more trouble with initiating new tasks, which can make it even more difficult to launch an advocacy platform than it would be for most other people. This has nothing to do with being lazy; it has to do with the fact that our brains have trouble with transitions. You might have heard this called 'executive dysfunction,' and it describes how our brains have trouble with starting new tasks, switching tasks, and staying focused on tasks. This product of our neurology can make it especially difficult to even get started as an advocate.

There are, however, some strategies to help you get the ball rolling. Once you have something - anything - it becomes much easier to keep going, because the ball, no matter how slowly at first, starts rolling down the hill. One of the easiest and most impactful early things you can do to build your platform is start a website. It could a blog, or a site full of information to advance your cause, or a directory to more information, or just a simple one-page site that explains briefly what your cause is and why you're passionate about it. Nowadays putting up a website is incredibly easy and can be done through a number of different hosting sites for free. As a first step I recommend you take 15 minutes and (with your parents' or guardians' permission if you are not yet an adult; see Chapter 6 for more information on staying safe online) register a website through an online provider of your choice. Don't worry about building your site or writing everything you want to say on it. Just go on, create an account, name your site, and create a URL.

Doing something as simple as starting a website can be very helpful in overcoming the initial inertia in starting a new advocacy platform because once a website is created, no matter how incomplete or preliminary, suddenly your idea for an advocacy platform exists somewhere outside of yourself. Even in the smallest way it is out there and in the world; it is real. Simply giving your platform, your goals, your site, or your movement a name can also be a powerful step towards getting started for the same reason: once something has a name, it becomes 'real' in a greater sense than if it were still just an abstract idea in your head, and therefore easier to act on.

Alright, so you've overcome the initial push, set up a website, given your platform a name, and outlined some of your early goals. You have a plan for how to start making a difference in your community. What comes next? When I first started writing on my current blog, I set small goals for myself to accomplish every week. I decided that I would write at least one blog post every week to be posted on Saturday and that I would fill out one page on my website every Wednesday. I broke down the task of launching my platform into manageable bite-sized bits to be accomplished over a longer period of time, all the while sharing what I had with the world to start building an audience and doing my best to make change in just a few people's lives, including my own.

For me this strategy worked perfectly, because the growth of my blog actually outpaced how quickly I could develop my platform. I had people asking where they could follow my blog on Twitter before I had created an account and people trying to get in contact with me before I had written anything on my 'contact' page. These small steps, baby steps if you will, provided enough momentum to get my platform off the ground and, most importantly, my message out into the world.

Therefore, I would recommend you set small, manageable weekly goals that help you advance your newly minted platform. Don't overwhelm yourself, but every week do your best to do something no matter how small so that you keep yourself engaged and lessen the risk of abandoning your advocacy platform before it even gets off the ground. I used my own website as an example but try to find ways to break down your own goals for building your platform, whatever that may be, into bite-sized, manageable bits. I call this the 'seize the day principle' because it involves making the most of each day by doing just one small thing that helps accomplish your long-term goals. By taking just one opportunity to seize the day every day you can complete even the largest of projects without overwhelming yourself.

Grow your platform slowly but consistently, and perhaps like me the growth of your influence will outpace the development of your platform! And let me tell you from experience, once you start seeing tangible results that confirm that your advocacy is making a real difference it is a very exciting feeling, and once you reach this point it becomes easy to continue expanding your influence and work as an advocate because it is very rewarding all in itself.

Self-advocacy

Finally, I want to talk just a little bit about self-advocacy. Self-advocacy is always an option for practicing your skills as an advocate and making your personal life better at the same time. Self-advocacy is the smallest form of advocacy, but don't confuse its small scale with it being unimportant! Even if you're not necessarily interested in advocating for a particular larger cause, it's still important to learn how to advocate for yourself and your needs as an autistic person. Unlike other forms of advocacy, self-advocacy is purely between yourself and those whom you directly interact with in your life: your family, your friends, your teachers and professors, your employer, your doctors, and other people who have a direct influence on your life.

Self-advocacy is ultimately no different than any other form of advocacy, except that what is being advocated for is your own needs, desires, and personal concerns. Because the focus of self-advocacy is you, its extent doesn't need to be any larger than your own personal sphere. The same techniques that can be used in larger-scale forms of advocacy can be applied to self-advocacy, but a self-advocacy platform only needs to be as large as the people you are personally connected to.

Because of its smaller, more manageable scale and because it's an important skill to develop anyway, self-advocacy can serve as a useful way to learn the skills necessary to launch a broader advocacy platform. Many young autistic advocates, whether they be autism advocates or advocates for a different cause, frequently report starting out as self-advocates and then growing their platform from there.

Remember in the last chapter when we were talking about being willing to stand up for your needs as part of embracing who you are? Well, this is essentially what self-advocacy is in a broad sense. An effective self-advocate will of course apply many of the techniques we'll talk about in this book, but in essence your goal as a self-advocate is to ensure your needs are acknowledged and accommodated, which is obviously important for us autistic people because very often we have different needs than many other people and so our needs may not be automatically accommodated by society like most people's are.

Being an effective advocate requires knowing your subject matter well, and as a self-advocate that subject matter is you. This sounds simple enough; after all who knows you better than yourself? This is true to a degree, as you are the world's foremost expert on what it's like to be you. However, interpreting your experiences and figuring out the answers to questions like 'What supports do I need in what circumstances?' and 'Why do I feel the way that I do?' is often much more difficult, and requires a significant amount of introspection or awareness of oneself. Unlike other subjects in which you can simply go online and read all you want about them, understanding yourself and your needs on a deep level is a skill that must be developed via practice.

One way that you can learn more about yourself is by journaling. Writing down, typing, or voice-recording your daily experiences and feelings can help you practice examining your own thoughts and emotions so that you can begin to gain a better awareness of your needs. A record of past experiences can also help you look for patterns and figure out what sorts of strategies and accommodations work best for you, what makes you feel calmer, and what things you might have difficulty with.

Another aspect of knowing yourself that should not be overlooked is knowing something about your sensory needs. Every second of every day your brain is taking in thousands of pieces of information from all of your senses, and it must sort through and integrate this sensory information. Your brain needs a certain amount of sensory input from each of your senses in order to operate optimally - not too much and not too little. The amount of sensory input your brain needs from your different senses is called your sensory profile. Imagine that your brain is like a bucket and sensory input is like water being poured into the bucket. Every day the bucket gets slowly filled up with water. If there's too much water the bucket will overflow, which is called sensory overload.

Everybody's 'bucket' is a different size, our sensory profiles are a little bit different, but for autistic people our sensory profiles are often narrower in terms of the amount of input we can work with because sometimes our brains have trouble integrating sensory information. I'll tell you from experience that balancing your daily sensory input according to your sensory profile is incredibly helpful in countless ways. Your sensory intake can have a massive impact on your mood, your energy, your executive functioning skills, your motor skills, and a variety of other areas in your life. This is why understanding your sensory profile and advocating for accommodations that help you stay regulated are so important.

For some people, journaling can again be helpful in figuring out what your sensory profile looks like. For many other people, however, it can be very difficult to determine in what areas you are more or less sensitive. Many autistic people have reported that they had lived for years in a near perpetual state of sensory overload and didn't realize it until they ended up burning out.

If you have trouble figuring out your sensory profile, try looking for patterns in how you feel after different types of sensory experiences. For example, if you suddenly feel very anxious or get very agitated after spending time in a crowded shop it might be a sign that you're sensitive to the sounds or lights or smells of the shop, and you might benefit from accommodations such as ear plugs or something similar. If everyday sensations are causing you any degree of discomfort or pain, even if it's temporary, this is also a sign that you're sensitive to that sense.

A lot of us have been taught since we were very little that we had to suppress sensory pain inside of us, and so you may not realize right away how much your senses are affecting you. You might be uncomfortable when a noise is too loud, or a light is too bright, or a smell is too strong, or a touch is too scratchy, but be fine a moment later. But every little sensation adds drops to the bucket, so even relatively 'minor' sensory sensitivities must be accounted for when trying to understand your sensory profile.

It's also possible that you could benefit from extra sensory input in certain areas. If I put a weighted blanket on my lap it can help me stay focused on a single task for longer (in fact I had a weighted blanket on my lap when I wrote this sentence!). Many people report feeling calmer after jumping on a trampoline, and some people may even feel more regulated and grounded after blasting loud music. Therefore, when thinking about your sensory profile - and how to accommodate your unique sensory needs - it is important to consider areas in which you may need both more stimulation and less stimulation.

I've been talking specifically about understanding your sensory needs because they are arguably one of the most important needs you have, and as an autistic self-advocate you will probably need to frequently advocate for the accommodation of your unique sensory profile. But there is of course much more to learn about yourself other than your sensory needs so that you can be an effective self-advocate. An entire other book could be written on self-exploration as an autistic young person. But for now, the best advice I can give to you is to learn from other autistic people. I learned a lot about myself from reading the blogs of other autistic people online, and this helped me know what could be done so that I was better supported, which gave me a better framework for knowing what I needed to self-advocate for.

In short, self-advocacy is no different than any other form

of advocacy. You can use all the same tools and techniques you would use for any other form of advocacy to advocate for yourself. The only major differences between self-advocacy and other forms of advocacy are in scale and subject matter. Self-advocacy is smaller in scope than other forms of advocacy because it need only reach those whom you are personally interacting with, and self-advocacy involves a subject matter that you can't just read about in a library book: you! But hopefully this section has given you a starting point towards discovering what your needs are and how to support these needs so that you can start to become a self-advocate.

Fortunately, there are many great organizations out there set up specifically to assist autistic self-advocates. Regardless of whether or not you want to build a dedicated platform around self-advocacy, it may be useful to do some research on autistic self-advocacy organizations both near you and around the world, as these can be great sources of information and support.

Concluding thoughts

So now after completing the steps in this chapter, you're officially on your way as an advocate. Congratulations! These first few steps may seem small, but they have laid the necessary groundwork to excel as an advocate and activist. Starting small will allow you to start making a difference without getting overwhelmed, all the while building skills and gaining experience that will make you a better advocate as your platform grows.

The next chapter will be all about communication: defining your message, looking at different methods of communication, ways of building up your platform, and how to be persuasive.

Interview 3: Clay on self-advocacy

Self-advocacy is an important skill for any autistic person to possess as we attempt to navigate the world and live our best lives. Even if you have no interest in any particular social cause or seeing any particular change advocacy skills can still be very important and useful when applied to yourself. Few people are likely to demonstrate this as well as the subject of our next interview: 19-year-old Clay Lewis from Queensland, Australia.

After Clay was unable to find an after-school job due to people in the area being resistant to hiring an autistic person, Clay started his own business, Clay's Bin Cleaning, which he has also been able to use as a platform to advocate for autism acceptance and fair hiring practices when it comes to autistic people.

What drove you to start your business? Had you always wanted to start your own business or was it a more 'spur of the moment' thing?

It was more from necessity actually. I had been looking for after-school work, applying for positions with the large retail stores and takeaway franchises, each time disclosing I was autistic as it's apparent I'm different. After not even receiving an interview I chatted with my parents and we came up with bin cleaning.

How have you been able to use your business as a self-advocacy platform? Can you recall any times that you needed to advocate for yourself in front of potential customers or other people in your life?

Fortunately, in the early days of my business I received a lot of media attention. I felt it was the perfect time to point out that I was hiring other kids from my school and meeting an important need of my community. That like most autistic people I had skills, capabilities, and potential. I challenged employers to look at their recruitment process and modify it to be more accommodating. I'm lucky that my community knows I'm autistic and are very supportive.

I also have had the chance to speak at both neurodiverse and neurotypical events, which gave me the chance to again send out a call to action to employers.

Starting a business or any other major project can be a huge undertaking. What strategies did you use to keep yourself motivated so you could get your business off the ground?

My mum has worked hard helping me in the early days. She was cleaning bins beside me and with the incremental training she gave me set me up for success. She did all the advertising, booking of appointments, and driving me around until I was able to get NDIS (National Disability Insurance

Scheme) funding to allow me to add a Support Worker to my team.

Do you think that self-advocacy is an important skill for autistic people to develop? If so, why?

Self-advocacy is a must. Our voices must be heard and amplified. We are the experts on our life. For example, even from the age of 13 there were elements of my life that my parents deferred to me on when important decisions needed to be made. I'm lucky that my mum is a big believer in the importance of self-advocacy and what youth have to offer.

What advice, if any, would you give to an aspiring young autistic advocate who wants to make change in the world?

You can do it. There are so many ways now to be heard. A non-speaking autistic person can make powerful TikTok videos. Or start in your school or community. Start with one person or a lot of people. What you have to say is important. Apply to youth parliament, create art or music. Do what matters to you in a way that matters to you.

Clay can be found online at the following:
Facebook: Clay Needs No Moulding and Clay's Bin Cleaning[2]
On the web: https://mmg-va.wixsite.com/claysbincleaning

---

2   www.facebook.com/clayisachamp

CHAPTER 4

Ways to Communicate

I can see myself now at 15, pacing back and forth in an empty classroom during lunch period, my head swimming with ideas and emotions all connected to my newfound desire to become an advocate. After doing more and more research on the neurodiversity paradigm and the autistic rights movement I felt like there was just a little bit more clarity in my life; I now had a framework to understand myself. I also had a set of ideas and principles that I felt strongly could be used to improve not only my own life but the lives of other autistic people as well.

I had started on a small scale by sharing my message on an unlisted blog to help the people in my life, but the more I wrote the more I desired to expand my advocacy platform to reach those outside of my own primary circle. Many of the struggles and trauma I experienced earlier in my childhood made sense as a symptom of the larger problem of a lack of understanding and acceptance of autism, and I was dead set to make my experience and knowledge heard so that at least one other autistic kid out there wouldn't have to go through the same things I went through.

The next thing I had to do was figure out what exactly it was that I wanted to tell the world based on what sorts of changes I wanted to see. I knew that I wanted people to better understand autism and embrace neurodiversity and autism acceptance so that autistic people would be treated better in the world. I knew that I wanted to combat ableism - discrimination against disabled people - both in my own communities and throughout the world. And finally, I knew that I wanted to connect with and share encouragement with fellow autistic people through shared experiences.

These are grand ideas, and in order to get them out into the world I needed some way of communicating and promoting them. And at this point on your journey as an advocate, this is likely to be your next step as well. You're excited about your topic, have an action plan for your advocacy platform, have your goals written down, and perhaps you've even taken the first steps to creating your platform. Now you'll need to build your platform by finding a way or several ways of communicating your ideas to the world to inspire change. This chapter is all about communication and how to 'find your voice.'

You see, the majority of your work as an advocate will be communicating with people. Sure, there are probably lots of things you can do by yourself to make change in your community, but to truly achieve your vision on a broad scale you will need to influence people through the communication of your message as an advocate. The purpose of communication as an advocate is to educate and persuade; that is, to inform your audience of your topic of choice and convince them to take action themselves. In fact, this is pretty close to the textbook definition of what an advocate is: one who openly supports and argues for a particular cause. In order for your ideas for a better world to take hold in your community you will need to convince a certain amount of people of your message and often even get them to change the way they think or act. This is not an easy feat, but this is why you're here reading this book. I assure you it is definitely doable, but I'll also be the first to tell you that advocacy isn't always easy.

If you think about it too hard, communication is kind of a strange thing. Communication is all about taking ideas that are in your own brain and then trying to upload those ideas into another person's brain by using external patterns, such as with the sounds that make up spoken language, the lines that make up written words, or any other forms of verbal and nonverbal signaling. There are almost as many ways to communicate as there are ideas to be communicated, and methods of communication are extensive.

This means that there are many different ways that you can get your message across and voice heard in your community. That's why the focus of this chapter will be communication: how to refine your message, build your platform with ways to communicate your message, and tips on how to become a more persuasive communicator.

What is your message?

Making change in the world is always a collective effort. Change in a community relies on most of the members of that community making a conscious decision to do differently; to do better. That's a big commitment for any one person to make, let alone most of a community. So, while there's a lot you can do personally to make a direct difference, much of your job as an advocate will involve convincing other people that change needs to be made and instructing them how to make that change.

Therefore, as an advocate you will be using your platform to advance your message. Your message is essentially what you are promoting as an advocate. It is the ideas that you are shouting out loud from your platform.

Your message as an advocate can ultimately be reduced down to communicating to others three things: calling out where change needs to occur, suggesting actions that should be taken, and looking forward to a better future if change occurs. Let's break down each of these three parts of your message and discuss why they are important to articulate.

CALLING OUT WHERE CHANGE NEEDS TO OCCUR

It's often said that the first step in fixing a problem is realizing that there is a problem. The thing is, while you might see very clearly that there is a problem and change is needed, many people will be completely oblivious to what you are advocating for. This is often simply because people don't have firsthand experience with your topic. As an example of this, if you're advocating for the protection of wildlife habitat from human encroachment, you might find that many people don't see this as a pressing issue simply because they live in cities away from open habitat. Similarly, autism advocates often find it difficult to get across the challenges that autistic people face in a world not designed for us simply because most people are not autistic, and even people who have experience of interacting with autistic people frequently do not have a very good understanding of autism.

Because of this disconnect, it is critical to make sure you specifically call out what issue you are looking to address and why. Never assume that people will have the same experiences you do or will have the same understanding of the problems you are trying to address. It may be necessary to make people a little bit uncomfortable with the way you present your message so that they may better understand the magnitude of the issue your community is facing and why change is desperately needed. It is important that you try to persuade people to be just as passionate about your topic of advocacy as you are. Your message should make people want to take action.

SUGGESTING ACTIONS THAT NEED TO BE TAKEN

One mistake that some advocates make is only bringing awareness to where change is needed but never suggesting what individual people can do to help address the problem. Bringing awareness to problems, calling out injustices, and highlighting where change is needed are important, but ultimately awareness is not enough. Your goal should be to encourage people to take action, and people can't take action if they don't know what to do, where to go, or how to start, no matter how passionate they are about your subject.

Further, if you focus only on a problem without presenting any solutions you risk simply depressing your audience rather than motivating them. Hope is a powerful motivating tool, and so suggesting actions to take can additionally help to spark passion and drive in your audience to want to personally make the world a better place, which is one of the biggest victories you can win as an advocate.

LOOKING FORWARD TO THE FUTURE

Human beings are neurologically hardwired to engage with stories, and as an advocate your overall message should tell a story following a hero arc of sorts. You begin by highlighting the way that things are and why change is needed, and then write a 'rising action' by advocating for the specific changes that need to be made to address the current state of affairs. Of course, every story needs a conclusion, and the conclusion in your message's 'story' comes in the form of looking towards a better future in which the changes you are advocating for have been made and the world is a better place because of it.

In addition to providing a sense of closure for your message, looking forward to a better future helps your audience understand the importance of your topic of advocacy and can help motivate them to take action in their daily lives. Despite the motivating power of a hopeful look at what could be, this piece is perhaps the most often left out of most advocates' messages. When caught up in the moment of advocating for change, it can be easy to forget that ultimately the goal of any advocate is to inspire enough change that advocacy is no longer necessary. Given just how much work there is to do in the world it's unlikely that this goal will ever be reached in a single lifetime, but the fact remains that advocacy is by definition a forward-thinking activity. It is of course important to acknowledge where we are now and call out what work needs to be done, but having a vision for what you want the future to look like is very important, and you should include this vision in your overall message.

Your message's key details

If you need, take some time right now to think about your message. Think about what changes you want to see in your community and why. Where and why is change necessary? How might people go about making this change? Should different groups of people respond differently to the problem? What would the world look like if what you are advocating for became a reality?

Break your message down into the three parts we just we just talked about. What do you have to say about your topic within each section? This may not come easy, and you may have to think really hard about exactly what it is you want to tell the world about what you're advocating for, but organizing your message this way will make your job much easier in the long run when you're promoting your message with your platform.

Having a good idea of the key details of your message is also important so that you can make your ideas simple. People are far more likely to engage with a topic if it is easy to understand. If you have to give a 30-minute presentation every time you want to tell someone about your message, then you haven't simplified it enough, and quite frankly your options for promoting your message will be very limited and you're going to lose most of your potential audience. People like to engage with things that are simple and easy to apply. Breaking down your message into simple small parts will broaden the range of ways you can promote your ideas and make your platform much more appealing.

Methods of communication

Once you have a good idea of what your message is, the next logical step is to figure out a way to communicate and broadcast this message out into the world. But how do you do this? How exactly is one supposed to build a platform from scratch, and what options are available for promoting your message? Luckily, there are probably just about as many ways to communicate your message as there are possible topics of advocacy, and even if you feel like you aren't particularly good at anything, when it comes to spreading your message there is inevitably a method out there somewhere that you can use to effectively communicate your advocacy to your audience.

As autistic people, we are somewhat stereotypically thought of as being poor communicators. However, I have found that this is not necessarily the case. I don't think that we lack communication skills, rather we have different communication skills. We are perfectly capable of expressing ourselves, but often to do this our communication needs to take a different route, whether it is for day-to-day purposes or for the purpose of promoting our message. Somewhere between 15 and 25 percent of us can't rely on speech as a method of reliable communication. Countless more of us find using traditional ways of communicating and expressing ourselves difficult. We autistics are therefore no strangers to creative means of communication.

The question to ask yourself then is not 'Am I able to communicate my message?' The question is 'What methodology will I use to communicate my message?' There are lots of different methods of communication that you can use to build your platform and promote your message.

Communication can be broadly grouped into verbal communication and nonverbal communication. Verbal communication includes anything that utilizes words while nonverbal communication includes anything that communicates without using words. There is a certain amount of semantic debate about whether or not 'verbal' refers only to spoken words or any sort of language usage at all, but for the purposes of this chapter 'verbal' will refer to anything that uses words in any way, including written words, while 'nonverbal' will refer to anything that doesn't use any words at all.

Verbal communication methods may seem like the most straightforward ways of promoting your message. You just write out or say exactly what you want your audience to know, right? Perhaps sometimes it is like this, but there are many more ways to communicate with words than with just straightforward writing or speaking. In fact, in many ways words can be seen as an artistic medium, with a blank page being no different than a blank canvas.

Similarly, though it may at first seem hard to get a specific idea across without using words, nonverbal communication can be an incredibly powerful way to promote your message and persuade your audience. The right photograph, a striking sculpture or painting, or an inspirational piece of music can all have a profound effect on your audience and help to promote change in the world.

Therefore, let's go over just a few of the ways that you might consider for promoting your message as an advocate.

NON-FICTION WRITING

Non-fiction writing is just about the broadest category of verbal communication we'll talk about, and it also may be the most straightforward way of communicating your message. If you didn't already know, non-fiction refers to any type of writing that is factual in nature. At first it may seem as though non-fiction writing leaves little room for creativity, but lots of different types of writing can be considered non-fiction so there are many ways to write factually while also expressing some creativity.

I've heard storytelling referred to as an art form, and telling true stories about yourself is certainly a form of non-fiction writing. I think it can be rather fun to tell personal stories; it's like trying to paint a picture with words so that the reader or listener feels like they were you in that moment. This is why storytelling about my experiences is one of my personal favorite forms of writing; it can be an entertaining puzzle trying to pick out and order the right words to try to give my audience some idea of what it was like to be in that moment. In my experience, people love to hear about other people's stories, so if you have a personal connection with your topic of advocacy then personal stories can be a great way to communicate your message.

Of course, sometimes you just need to bluntly get the facts out there, especially if you're under a time limit or word count limit. In cases like this it's useful to be able to communicate the facts in a straightforward manner, so if you don't think you're very good at extended, flowery writing just remember that being blunt is a skill too. There is no right or wrong way to communicate so long as it gets your intended message out there.

In fact, there's a concept out in the business world called the 'elevator pitch' that can be useful in an advocacy context as a short piece of non-fiction writing (or speaking). An elevator pitch in this context is what you would, hypothetically, tell someone about your advocacy work if you had to do it while riding in an elevator: about 30 seconds or 100 words in writing. Being able to condense the three parts of your message (calling out where change is needed, suggesting actions to be taken, and looking forward to the future) into a 30-second pitch is very handy in a variety of situations. It's something you can put on the 'about' page of a blog or in the description of a social media page, and you can even memorize it as a script for when people ask you on-the-fly what your advocacy work is about.

Knowing the main ideas of your message to the point that you can condense them down into an elevator pitch can also be a good exercise for coming to a better understanding of your topic in general, because it makes you think about what the underlying big ideas of your message and advocacy work are. And, hey, it's not uncommon for us autistics to be super knowledgeable about narrow topics, so perhaps we have the 'upper hand' when it comes to being able to write an elevator pitch for our message, and generally when it comes to non-fiction writing as a communication method.

POETRY

When you think of poetry you might think of almost incomprehensible Shakespearean plays or of trying to come up with two words that rhyme, but in reality, poetry is simply structured writing with a specific rhythm that is designed to convey a specific emotion or set of emotions. There aren't any specific rules you have to follow when writing poetry; it doesn't have to rhyme or follow any specific rhythm. You can quite literally make up the rules as you go along ('free verse' poetry). So although poetry may seem fancy and complicated, don't discount it as a way you could potentially spread your message, as it's a lot more accessible than you might imagine. You're probably exposed to poetry on an almost daily basis, as most song lyrics are written poetically. If you're a little bit intimidated by the prospect of writing poetry, try thinking of poetry as written song lyrics.

Poetry is unique among forms of writing in that it is especially suited to being used to convey emotional ideas. There's something about the rhythmic structure combined with the word choice of the poet that helps the reader connect with the emotions being conveyed in the poem. Poetry can help your audience connect with a different perspective and understand other viewpoints. For these reasons, poetry can be a powerful tool through which you can convey your message, and indeed many advocates have used poetry very effectively to promote their message and inspire change in the world. Why not give it a shot? You might find that poetry can help you express all kinds of ideas, and you may have fun doing it as well.

COMEDY

Comedy might seem like a rather strange means of communicating about your advocacy message. Your topic is probably very serious with very important, real-world consequences, and it might be difficult to see how joking and laughing can convey a serious message. But what gives comedy potential for promoting an advocacy message is that it can allow people to connect with a serious subject in a light-hearted way. Approaching a subject in a comedic way can make people more willing to think about it and deal with it, and well-written comedy can be used to point out injustices and areas of urgently needed change in an engaging way.

PUBLIC SPEAKING

Public speaking is another broad category of verbal communication that can cover anything from casually talking to a few people to giving a formal presentation in front of a large audience. As an advocate, it is likely that at some point you will have to do some public speaking, and you may even want to because presenting in front of an audience is a fantastic way to promote your message.

However, public speaking can be a little bit of a difficult topic for some autistic people, including myself, largely because if you've ever taken a public-speaking class or done some research on how to be a good public speaker it seems like all the advice that is given goes directly against autistic neurology. The importance of eye contact is often stressed, as is the 'correct' neurotypical expression of body language, making the correct movements, tone of voice, and vocal rhythm, all of which can be difficult to focus on when your brain isn't wired to make your body work this way. Not to mention the fact that many of us have at least some degree of difficulty with speech itself.

Here we're going to focus entirely on public speaking from the autistic perspective; I'm not here to coach you on making eye contact, holding your body a certain way, and making your voice sound the right way. What's more important than appearing a specific way while you speak is your actual message itself, and if trying to meet some body language or vocal standard is distracting you from getting your message across, then I would advise you to not worry so much about it. After giving a speech or presentation people are much more likely to remember the quality of your message rather than if you had the right body language or not. Plus, I would argue that it's really not a fair standard to expect everyone to show a specific neurotypical display of body language, so I would encourage you not to feel pressured into public speaking in a way that is uncomfortable, unnatural, or stressful for you.

Another interesting little hint about public speaking is that, technically speaking, it doesn't actually require, well, speaking. I know, I know, this sounds like an outright contradiction, but public speaking is essentially about spontaneously communicating your message to an audience in person, and this can be accomplished without speaking on the spot. I have been to symposiums before where some presenters chose to pre-record a video presentation, show the video during their presentation time, and then field questions afterwards.

Also, if you are a person who communicates through a means other than speaking (such as AAC: 'augmented alternative communication') you can use your preferred method of communication to present your message. If you are capable of speech but find it difficult in the context of public speaking it might also be a good idea to present using a communication method that does not involve speaking (such as typing, using text-to-speech programs, pointing to letters, showing a pre-recorded video presentation, etc.).

Another thing that can make public speaking difficult is that a lot of people have anxiety around the idea of speaking in front of strangers, even if the audience is small. This is a very common fear, and in certain people it can be debilitating. I have personal experience with this anxiety. I've been in the middle of presentations where I have had to take a long pause because I was so nervous it was almost like I had forgotten how to speak.

Overcoming anxiety and phobias is a complex topic that I'm not really qualified to write about beyond sharing my personal experience, so that's what I will do. Typical advice you'll hear like 'imagine the audience is in their underwear' has never been helpful for me, nor do I dwell too much on being laughed off the stage or anything of that nature. The only specific worry I can remember having sometimes is whether I'll be able to deliver the presentation or speech; other than that I get nervous for seemingly no specific reason, which is pretty standard when it comes to anxiety it seems.

What I've done in the past to make it through a speech or

presentation I'm anxious about is to type out exactly what I'm going to say beforehand and focus simply on reading out loud what's on the page. It helps me to sort of 'zone out' while I'm speaking, and I always get into a rhythm of reading a few sentences to a paragraph, glancing up towards the audience, and then continuing. This has helped me mask my anxiety while public speaking, and I've never heard anything other than good feedback for my presentations and speeches.

If, however, you have so much anxiety around the idea of public speaking that it's causing you distress or you aren't sure of your ability to give a speech or presentation, even in front of a small audience, then perhaps public speaking isn't the correct medium for sharing your message. But that's totally okay! There is no one set correct way to spread your message; no one set correct way to be an advocate. It is always okay to focus your energy somewhere that is less stressful for you in order to more fully embrace and exploit your strengths.

PODCASTS

Podcasts are a great option for spreading your message because they're essentially a form of public speaking but without the public part and also have the benefit of being available on the internet where information can spread quickly due to social media. Podcasts have become increasingly popular over the last few years because they're a time-accessible way of consuming media for people living increasingly busy lives. Therefore, podcasts offer a fantastic opportunity through which to get your advocacy message out into the world.

Podcasts can be created singly or in an episodic format,

sort of like an audio blog. If you have access to a microphone there are several places where you can create and upload podcast episodes for free, making it a fairly easy medium to get started in. And while the 'standard' way of creating a podcast would be to speak out loud into a microphone, just like with public speaking it is possible to create a podcast without needing to actually speak if you think this would be a challenge for you. You can have someone else read a script you wrote, for example, or a script could be put into speech-generating software, making podcasts a very accessible form of communicating your message.

MEMES

If one thing had to be used to describe our generation, it may very well be meme culture. If you've spent even a little bit of time on the internet in the past ten years then the chances are very good that you *know* what a meme is, even if it's somewhat hard to describe what exactly a meme *is*. Memes might be the most popular way to share information over the internet right now, because of their ease of sharing and appealing format, so memes present an excellent means of reaching lots of people with basic ideas about your message. In fact, I think that the meme is perhaps the greatest advocacy tool that has ever come into existence; it is that powerful for spreading easy-to-understand ideas to lots of people.

A meme is, at its core, a bite-sized idea shared over the internet in an often humorous or relatable way. Memes are typically images or short videos but can really be any form of media so long as it is shared widely among internet users.

Memes are generally light-hearted, but this does not mean they cannot be used to address very serious problems; in fact part of the appeal of some memes is the fact that they comment on relatable and important issues in a way that makes people think due to their humorous or unexpected nature.

There is huge potential to have a big influence through creating memes. Memes can be used to creatively spread little bits and pieces of your message at a time in a way that they will resonate with a wide variety of people. Creating a meme page on a social media site is a perfectly valid way of advocating, and for many people can be very fun as well.

DRAMA AND THEATER

One unique way you could communicate your message is through the performing arts. You could write a script for a play that deals with your topic of choice and features your advocacy message and then perform it with your friends and family. Make sure you record the performance so you can put it up online! Or if you're already involved with (or want to get involved with) the world of theater perhaps you could eventually perform your play with a theater club or at school.

VISUAL ARTS

Painting, drawing, sculpting, graphic design, and photography are all art forms that fall within the visual arts, which are of course any artistic media that is experienced primarily through vision, which is pretty self-explanatory given the name. Some of the world's most forward-thinking ideas have been promoted through visual media. When done well, the visual arts can be used to get your audience reflecting on new concepts, which is precisely your goal as an advocate.

The right photograph can be very effective when it comes to highlighting where change needs to occur. Provocative photos of elephants killed by poachers and war-torn cities are classic examples of how a visual artform has been used to motivate people to take action for a particular cause. You too might try your hand at using drawing, photography, or another visual artform to highlight where change needs to occur in your community.

MUSIC

I have been a music lover for a very long time now, and one of the things that I love the most about music is its ability to evoke palpable emotions almost instantly in the listener and use these emotions in combination with lyrics to comment on complex issues and topics. Music is an artform that has tied humanity together for centuries; many people have an almost spiritual connection with music. This makes music perfectly suited for communicating your advocacy message if you enjoy making music.

Typically, when we think of communicating through music we tend to think of lyrics, which are generally just poetry set to music. Song lyrics have been used to great effect in the past to communicate an advocacy message. In fact, some music genres, such as rap, started with people using a genre's lyrics to advance a specific cause or bring attention to injustice in the world. In the case of lyrics, communicating your message through music is very similar to communicating your message through poetry, which we discussed earlier.

But what makes music so special is that it has the capacity to act as a method of communication not just through lyrics, but through the notes themselves. Music by itself can make us feel different things, and so music can be paired with its lyrics to communicate verbally to a listener while also infusing that message with an emotional backdrop. Instrumental music by itself can go a long way towards telling a story or communicating a specific feeling, which can help you evoke the sorts of emotions that are necessary for your listener to fully understand your message.

If you can sing or play an instrument (or want to learn how to sing or play an instrument) then making music can be a fantastic way for you to communicate your message as an advocate. And even if you don't know how play an instrument there are many different pieces of software out there that can be used to compose music without having to know how to play anything. Different genres of music are better for conveying different types of emotions, so it might be worthwhile to do a little bit of experimenting to figure out what types of music are best suited to communicating your particular message. If you're really interested in music, it might also be worth taking a class or doing some online research into music theory to discover how to write music in order to evoke specific emotions within your listener.

Thanks to modern technology, it is possible to record and mix music at a fairly decent sound quality with minimal, relatively inexpensive equipment. Original music can also be published online for free through websites like Bandcamp and YouTube. This makes music an accessible way to promote your advocacy message if you enjoy music composition and production.

FILM AND VIDEO PRODUCTION

Lots of people rely on watching videos and movies as both their primary form of entertainment and of obtaining new information. Video production can therefore be a very effective means of getting your message out into the world. Making short videos or vlogs that detail the different aspects of your message, your various thoughts on your topic of advocacy, and why you're passionate about your topic of advocacy can be a fun way to reach lots of new people with your voice as an advocate.

You can really let your creativity flow when planning, shooting, and editing videos to make them informative and entertaining. An advocacy message can also be spread through fictional videos, such as through skits that demonstrate or highlight one part of your message. I know of advocates that have even used self-produced, full-length movies or documentaries to promote their cause. The possibilities when it comes to film and video production are nearly endless!

Finished videos can be uploaded to dedicated video-streaming websites like YouTube or TikTok, and can then be embedded on just about any website, which makes them very easy to share. A YouTube channel or something similar could even serve as your 'home base' as an advocate if video production becomes your primary method of sharing your message and inspiring change.

Communication your way

There's a chance that right now you're feeling a little bit apprehensive. You might be thinking to yourself, 'Well, what if I'm just not good at any of these?' If this is you, I want you to remember a few things:

First, remember that these are only a few of many different ways to communicate your message and there are countless other methods of communication that have been used to great effect by advocates in the past. If there's a way you would feel more comfortable expressing yourself than those listed here, then you should totally go for it. It's most important that you are comfortable with whatever way you decide to let your voice be heard than that you use any specific method of communication.

Second, remember that you don't need to be the world's greatest writer, or poet, or speaker, or film director, or musician, or anything else in order to be a good advocate. What's important is that you have an outlet through which your message can influence people and advocate for change. So don't be concerned about whether you're 'good enough' or anything like that; go for it! You might be pleasantly surprised with the results. And, finally, it may take a little bit of experimentation to find what sort of medium works well for you, so never be afraid to branch out and try new ways of communicating and advocating.

Promoting your voice

Once you have found a method (or several methods) of communicating your message, the next step is to find a way to get it out into the world. Think of it like this: you can go out into the wilderness and scream as loud as you want, but it won't have any impact on anybody if nobody is around to hear it. You can be the best writer, artist, public speaker, or director in the world, but if you can't get anybody to come to see your finished product then it's not going to have any impact on anybody and is therefore useless for the purpose of advocacy.

If the scale of your target audience is small, say if you are a self-advocate or are otherwise only interested in spreading your message to people you personally know, then promoting your voice is fairly straightforward. You can simply reach out to people you know in person or through email, social media, or another messaging service and say, 'I think reading this will help you understand me better' or 'I'd really like you to consider this' before sharing your work with them. However, if you're looking to reach people you don't necessarily know personally, then you'll have to find a means of getting your message out into the world and promoting your voice.

Promoting your message and platform is just as important as how you decide to communicate your message. Luckily, with the advent of the internet and especially social media, it is easier than ever to promote your message to your intended audience. I have seen firsthand how one person's blog post or video has gone 'viral' and impacted countless people, and it is also very true that a single person (such as you) has the capacity to make a widespread change within a community if their message is promoted and delivered correctly.

I will warn you however that whatever method or methods you choose to utilize to promote your voice it is very easy to lose sight of your original purpose as an advocate: inspiring change in your community, and perhaps even throughout your country and the world. It's easy to become distracted by viewership statistics or accumulating more likes, follows, and shares to the point that you forget what purpose your goal is as an advocate – to influence people in order to create change – which ultimately can be accomplished just as well with ten followers as it can be with 10,000 followers. It is not the size of your advocacy platform that matters, it is what impact you have over the audience you do have. Focusing on inspiring change among the audience you *do* have is what is most important, and really if you have a compelling enough message your audience will naturally grow over time.

I'll tell you from past experience that when something you've made goes big or 'viral' on the internet it's a very exciting feeling. It's easy to lose sight of your goal of making change and start creating content just to gain more viewers or followers rather than to advance your cause. There have been times where I have briefly forgotten that I'm writing my blog to make the world a better place for autistic people rather than just writing to accumulate views and followers.

So, with that out of the way, let's go over a few of the different ways you can promote your communication about your topic, shall we?

BLOGGING

A blog is essentially a website where you post shorter pieces of writing in the format of dated entries or posts. Blogging is an incredibly open-ended way to share your message via writing, and I suggest that every aspiring advocate create a blog. It can be done for free, once created can be easily shared, and can grow with your platform. I got my own start in advocacy from blogging, and whatever you're advocating for or whatever your topic is, I cannot recommend enough that you create a blog and at least try to post something on it semi-regularly.

A blog can also serve as a sort of 'headquarters' for your advocacy platform, as you can put all sorts of information about yourself and your advocacy work on it. You can create an 'about me' page where your audience can learn a little more about you and why you're passionate about your advocacy work (just make sure you don't reveal so many details that it becomes unsafe!). You can post links to your platform's social media accounts and additional resources so your audience can learn more. A blog has power not only to promote your written words, but to be a central hub that connects your entire platform.

Typically, it is verbal communication that is posted on a blog. Informational posts, personal stories, calls to action, status updates, reviews, poetry, screenplays, and all other types of verbal communication will find a blog a suitable home, but you can use a blog to promote your nonverbal communication as well. Pictures and videos can also work well in a blog format, allowing you to use your blog to promote all your communication as an advocate.

SOCIAL MEDIA

Social media is just about the fastest and easiest way to promote just about anything these days. Almost everyone is on some form of social media, and the computer-generated algorithms keep curated content pumping through everyone's feeds. This is the perfect environment to spread your message as an advocate, and indeed many advocates have inspired massive change using only social media.

Even if you aren't on social media now, it's not a bad idea to set up a few pages for your advocacy platform. I wasn't really active on social media until I became an advocate, and even now there are many platforms that I don't have a personal account for, only an account for my advocacy, so it's alright if you don't have any previous experience with social media.

If you do have your own personal social media account or accounts, I recommend you don't use them as the official pages for your advocacy platform. This is mostly for privacy purposes, but also because it allows for a separation between your personal life and your advocacy work, which can sometimes be a huge mental health saver. On some social media sites such as Facebook you can create a 'page' for your advocacy platform that can be controlled by your own personal account.

Social media also offers a great opportunity for you to connect and network with other advocates in your field and is a great place to build community and receive support (just make sure you are always extremely cautious when interacting with anybody over the internet). Connecting with other advocates is a fantastic first step to getting your message heard and your voice out into the world, as advocates are generally very inclined to amplify the voices of our allies through shares and comments.

Like blogging, social media is also a very versatile way to share the work you are doing to spread your message. Certain social media platforms are more geared towards one particular type of media (YouTube is geared towards videos, Instagram is geared towards pictures, etc.) while others are more general in what can be shared on them, but just about any social media site can be used to share your work and spread your message to a broad audience.

LEAFLETS, POSTERS, AND FLYERS

As we already explored earlier, your advocacy platform should initially aim to create relatively small-scale change on a localized level, such as among your family, within your school, and within your town or city. Early on this is where your platform has the potential to make the biggest impact, and you can always broaden your horizons as your audience grows. While the promotion of your platform via the internet is versatile enough to be useful on both a smaller and larger scale, when it comes to spreading your message within your local communities there is little that can make as much of an impact as a good ol' stack of papers and a stapler.

Posters, pamphlets, leaflets, flyers, and other forms of paper communication can be created by hand or created digitally and then printed. Writing and visual arts are especially suited to communication via poster or pamphlet. However, what can be difficult about physical media is that it requires a physical space to be shared, and the majority of public physical spaces are probably owned by someone else who may not want flyers or posters tacked on to their property.

The good news is there are a few places where you may have better luck acquiring permission to put up flyers or posters. If you attend an in-person school you might approach your school's dean, principal, or headteacher and ask if you can put up a few posters around the school. This is an especially good place to start if you're advocating for a topic that would be applicable to your peers, such as mental health advocacy or anti-bullying advocacy.

In some places you can put up flyers on certain public objects such as street posts, but you should check your local ordinances before attempting to put anything up on public property. Also, consider that it may not be the most efficient use of your resources to just put up flyers in random locations. Generally, you will get more engagement from your audience if you target your platform a bit, so unless your topic of advocacy is something that is important for and applicable to just about everybody in your community there are probably better uses of time than randomly putting up posters and flyers around town.

One of the more impactful ways I have seen paper flyers and leaflets used by advocates in the past is at protests. I have seen people at protests handing out informational flyers to passers-by to inform about why they are protesting, why it is important, and how to get involved with the movement.

Passing out informational flyers in situations such as this is a great way to quickly reach local people and communicate your message to them.

COMMUNITY ADVOCACY EVENTS

Unless your topic of advocacy is unusually niche, limited in scope, or only applicable on a very small local scale, you are very unlikely to be alone as an advocate. Chances are there are lots of other advocates out there who are working to bring about the same types of change in the world that you are, and there may even be a few that live in the same area as you do.

One of my favorite parts about being an advocate is meeting and interacting with other advocates both online and in-person. I have found that there are often many opportunities to network and share ideas with other advocates, and such events can be great places to share your work with others and hopefully gain a little bit of promotion from established advocates.

PUBLIC FORUMS AND COMMENTS

In many places, local governments will frequently hold public meetings, public forums, or opportunities for open public comment so that they can hear input from the community and better serve the citizens in their jurisdiction. These provide excellent opportunities for your voice to be heard by your local government officials and can be a great way to inspire change in your local community. Sometimes these events pertain to a specific topic or proposal and sometimes they are open to whatever comments members of the public want to make. Keep an eye out for dates of public city council or town hall meetings, public forums, and open comment sessions that you can attend to get the attention of your local public officials. Just keep in mind that often your opportunity for comment is short, so be ready to get what you want to say across in only a few minutes.

If you cannot attend one of these events or speaking in public is inaccessible for you, you can also try directly contacting your local (and perhaps even national) elected officials through letters or email. This is an opportunity to pitch your message to people who have the power to directly influence legislation, and so can be a very fruitful way to help impact change as an advocate.

Crafting your message

When you get into the flow of doing advocacy work it can sometimes be difficult to remember your bottom line; that is, your ultimate goal as an advocate: inspiring change. The very reason why you would go out of your way to actively promote any cause or idea is because you want to see real change in your community, in your country, and even throughout the world.

Therefore, your platform should not only raise awareness about and public knowledge of your topic, it should also aim to convince people of the importance of your topic so that they start making real changes in their life. This is a lot harder than it sounds because people are more inclined to keep doing things the way they have always done them, even if they are aware it is harmful, than to go out of their way to make changes in their life. The good news is that there are ways that you can craft your methods of communication and outreach, whatever they may be, in order to inspire others to take action.

Luckily, there are ways to fine tune the way you deliver your message so that it has a bigger impact on your audience and inspires more change. The biggest way to amplify the impact of your message is through the application of rhetoric. Rhetoric is essentially the art of persuasion. In the context of an advocacy platform, it is presenting your information in such a way that people are both persuaded and inspired to take action and make changes in their day-to-day lives.

Rhetorical persuasion is usually classified into three different modes: pathos, ethos, and logos. Each of these modes involves a different way of persuading people to think a specific way or take a specific action. Let's take a look at each of these:

Pathos is the emotional appeal. It's all about creating an emotional response within your audience and then using these strong emotions to motivate your audience to take a specific action or persuade them to think a certain way. A great example of pathos is often seen in television commercials for animal shelters. The ad will show pictures of sad-looking puppies and kittens while playing sad music and asking for donations so you can help give the poor animals a good home. These types of commercials rely strongly on pathos by trying to use their viewers' empathy and emotional connection to animals to persuade them to donate.

One of the best ways to use pathos when communicating your message is to tell stories. People are generally hardwired to emotionally connect with a story, and a story can be put to good use by an advocate when it exposes an injustice or demonstrates a problem. Pathos can also be incorporated into your message with the use of emotionally charged words. It's one thing to say that something is 'bad'; it's quite another to say that something is 'horrendous' or 'sickening.' The last two words are much more emotionally dense, and by using charged words such as these you can inspire a greater emotional response in your audience and make them more likely to take action or think differently.

Ethos is the ethical appeal, otherwise known as the appeal from authority. It involves the testimony of people who are in a position of authority or have experience within a topic. Have you ever seen ads that say something like 'nine out of ten dentists recommend toothpaste brand XYZ'? Well, those ads are an example of ethos, because they are taking the testimony of people experienced within the field of tooth care and using it to try to persuade their audience into buying their toothpaste brand. Ethos is also often seen in things like celebrity endorsements and product placement, whereby when people see someone famous or recognizable doing a certain thing or using a certain product they are more likely to take that action or use that product.

One way that I frequently see ethos being used by advocates, even on a smaller scale, is through surveys. I will often see autism and neurodiversity advocates in my circles taking surveys through social media in order to gather information like '92 per cent of autistic people surveyed said they prefer the use of identity-first language over person-first language.' Using this survey data as a persuasive technique counts as ethos because it's using the opinions of people who have experience in a particular area in order to lend credibility to a particular idea.

Surveys and interviews are some of the easiest ways you can incorporate ethos into your message and platform. For example, if you're preparing to give a speech in front of your city council, why not first interview people in your community who are impacted by the topic you're advocating for and then use their testimony to try to persuade your local leaders to take action?

Logos is the logical appeal, and it focuses on data, statistics, scientific studies, experiments, reasoning, and empirical evidence. It's about presenting hard facts and drawing logical conclusions to persuade your audience. The use of logos is generally pretty straightforward, involving the citing of scientific studies and data or walking one's audience through a set of logical steps.

The use of logos can also occasionally be seen in advertising when an 'experiment' is performed on-screen, such as a paper towel commercial that aims to prove its brand is the best by showing how it absorbs more than its competitors, or a commercial for a brand of duct tape that proves its effectiveness when it is used to patch a large hole in a tank of water. In both of these cases the logical conclusion of an experiment is being relied upon to try to persuade viewers to take the action of buying the particular product being advertised.

The use of logos to promote your own message is generally also fairly straightforward assuming you can find the correct sources. With the internet it is easier now than at any time in history to access scholarly information for use in a logical appeal. Resources like Google Scholar make finding peer-reviewed published information on just about any topic very accessible. Sometimes a single reference to a peer-reviewed paper can turn a barely persuasive argument into a rock-solid case that will inspire the change you wish to see in the world.

Now, it is unfortunately true that many publications can only be accessed with a paid journal subscription, but I'll let you in on a little secret: if you send an email to the person who wrote the paper and ask nicely, they will very often be willing to send you a PDF copy of the paper for free. Researchers generally do not directly benefit from publication paywalls, and they also generally want their research to be read by as many people as possible, so many are more than happy to give you access to their work so you can use it to support your advocacy platform.

Once you can recognize these three modes of persuasion, you'll start to see them everywhere, such as in advertising, in speeches, and in persuasive newspaper and internet articles. And you can use them too to make a greater impact with whatever format you decide to use to promote your message.

Every person is different, and the three different rhetorical modes will be more or less impactful to each individual person because of differences in personality. Therefore, it's generally advisable to try to use each of the three rhetorical modes when you're trying to persuade an audience to think a certain way or take a certain action. When I'm writing a persuasive blog post or making a persuasive speech, I intentionally make sure to work in persuasive elements using pathos, ethos, and logos. I will intentionally use pathos by choosing to use emotionally charged words or tell an emotionally charged story. I will intentionally use ethos by using a quote from a prominent figure. I will intentionally use logos by citing a scientific study. Mentally acknowledge that you are using a specific rhetorical mode each time you work it into your content.

Every method of communication listed in this chapter can be used persuasively, but of course some ways of communicating your message are better suited towards integrating certain rhetorical modes than others. For example, music is heavily geared towards pathos because it is good at creating a strong emotional response in listeners. Depending on how you are getting your message out into the world you may lean more heavily on one rhetorical mode than others.

The communication slog

Finally, I would like to acknowledge that communication as an advocate can sometimes be a difficult job. You will frequently find yourself in situations that can be frustrating, such as when it seems like people just aren't understanding your message, when it feels like you're just not 'getting through,' or when people misrepresent what you say to fit their narrative. This is especially the case if your topic of choice is particularly controversial, no matter how good your intentions are. You might also find that you're answering the same questions repeatedly, which can quickly become exhausting. This was actually part of what inspired me to write some of my earliest public blog posts: I was bringing up the same concepts or answering the same questions over and over and I found it was much easier just to link to a blog article than explain it every time.

It is important though that no matter how many times you have to say the same thing, no matter how many seemingly stupid questions you get asked, or no matter how mind-numbingly ignorant someone seems on your topic, you continue to put yourself out there rather than throw your arms up in frustration and give up. Treat every opportunity for communication as an opportunity to persuade, if not the person you're directly interacting with then the people silently watching your interaction or listening to the way you're presenting your message. On the other hand, remember that your own mental health is important, and it's never worth it to argue your way into a shutdown, so make sure you take care of yourself as well when advocacy becomes tedious, overwhelming, or frustrating.

You should always aim to be assertive when communicating your advocacy message, no matter what medium of communication you choose. Don't resort to using insults and personal attacks against anyone, but at the same time don't let anyone bully you into compromising on your message or your advocacy platform. When the going gets tough and communication becomes frustrating just remember that even though it may not seem like it, just by getting your voice out into the world you will have an influence on your audience, and slowly you can help to bring about the change you wish to see in the world.

Concluding thoughts

Activism is centered around your voice, which is promoted by your platform, which is built up by your methods of communication. Communication is essential to being an advocate and finding a method or methods of communication that you are comfortable expressing yourself through is among the most important parts of your platform. By making your message heard you can be an influence for positive change.

Now that the foundations of your advocacy platform have been laid down and solidified, it's time to start putting your voice to use and advancing your cause. The next chapter will focus on managing and growing your platform: staying safe, marketing yourself, managing mental health, and dealing with criticism.

Interview 4: Tom on communication

Finding a method of communication that suits you well is a critical part of being an advocate. That's why our next interview features none other than the superb 'Autastic' Tom, 23-year-old self-advocate from the United States and creator of the Autastic Tom video series on YouTube. Tom uses his videos to teach others more about autism and autistic people, and how best to support us. Tom produces his videos by writing out the script beforehand and then recording himself presenting out loud what he has written. He has also written and performed an original intro-jingle for his video series. Because Tom has found several creative ways to use different types of media to communicate his message, there is likely much to be learned from him.

In 2018 you started posting videos you had made online. What made you want to start making videos for the Autastic Tom YouTube channel?

Really, the most important thing for me was for people to see that individuals who don't speak reliably have a lot to say. I talk a lot; however, the words aren't what I want to say. When I spell or type I am able to communicate my true thoughts. Starting Autastic Tom on YouTube was a way to show the world that nonspeakers are some smart and funny individuals.

Every advocate has a message or set of ideas they want to share with the world. How would you summarize your message, and how did you decide that this is what you wanted to advocate for?

That's a great question. Simply put, nonspeaking does not equal nonthinking. It was something that many had communicated that they felt about me through how they spoke to me, and no one should be subjected to that, including individuals with other disabilities. My hope is that through watching my videos people will think about how they address people like me.

Your videos have proven to be a great way for you to communicate with the world about autistic people and how to support us. Are there any other ways that you have been able to communicate your message to others, either verbally or nonverbally? Which communication method have you found to be the most effective?

Yes, I have been able to communicate my message in other forums. I have spoken at conferences, and I have recently helped to educate others by writing brochures with other nonspeakers about how to support us. However, my true thoughts only come out on a letterboard or a keyboard.

I imagine that sometimes it can be very difficult to convince some people of what you have to say, which can certainly be very frustrating. Have you ever used any persuasive techniques in the past to try to convince more people of what you're trying to teach the world, or do you think it's better to just ignore the nay-sayers altogether?

It tests my patience to really try to engage with the haters or nay-sayers as you call them, so I fairly often will disengage from those conversations. They will eventually realize that I was right.

What advice, if any, would you give to an aspiring young autistic advocate who wants to make change in the world?

I long to have more young self-advocates. I want to think that those people who started before them will make it easier, having paved the way. My advice I want to give is to try to really have your words be words that come from your heart. People love to listen when someone is passionate about what they are saying.

Tom can be found online at the following:
Facebook: Autastic Tom[1]
YouTube: Autastic Tom[2]

1   www.facebook.com/autastictom
2   www.youtube.com/channel/UC9_5hv5v8IHcbNPgrJvdNMQ

CHAPTER 5

Growing Your Audience

One of the most exhilarating experiences that ever happened to me on my advocacy journey occurred less than a month after I had launched my public blog, back at the very beginning of 2019. I woke up on a cold February morning before school and, as I always impulsively do, checked the notifications on my phone. I was surprised to find over two dozen notifications from Wordpress, the website through which I host my blog. It turned out that the blog post that I had launched the night before, which I thought had been a fairly standard article about supporting autistic people like me, had amassed tens of thousands of views over a single night.

So what happened? Well, the day before I had posted the link to the new blog post in a neurodiversity-centered Facebook group, where one of the members who ran a large-scale autism advocacy page enjoyed the post and decided to share it. And from that point on it was an exponential domino effect. I watched as my blog went viral through the autistic community and beyond. I spent the entire day feeling like I was floating on a cloud as I watched the emails, comments, and shares roll in.

What caught me off guard though was that my reach as an advocate had rapidly outpaced the size of my platform. At the time I only had my blog website and my personal Facebook account through which I occasionally shared articles in groups and with my friends, but that day people kept asking me how they could follow me on Twitter or if I had an email list before I had even finished setting up my website's 'about' page. So, I rapidly went about creating a Twitter account, polishing up the look of my blog, and creating a Facebook page to center my platform around. At this point I was just trying to keep up with my own growth!

The best part about seeing my blog go viral was the connections I made with other autism advocates around the world. I watched as names that I recognized, people whose advocacy I had followed for years and whose writings had shaped much of my thought around neurodiversity, complimented my writing and followed my blog pages on social media. Even though I was a newcomer in the world of autism and neurodiversity advocacy I felt like I had become a legitimate advocate; like I was finally part of the movement that I had spent so long reading about.

That's my story anyway, how I went from shouting into the metaphorical void to feeling like I had a voice that could be heard as an autism advocate. But of course, everyone's journey will be different, so let's talk about what may come next for you as a new advocate. At this point, if you've been following along, you should be at a place where you have the foundations for your advocacy platform in place. You've identified your topic and your message. Hopefully you have a plan for what methods you're going to use to communicate your message, and you may have even started on building your platform through the creation of a website, a social media page, or something similar. What comes next then is the fun part: putting yourself out there, promoting your ideas, and, well, simply being an advocate.

Putting yourself out there

If you feel like you're ready, it's time to go ahead and take your first action as an advocate and activist. Write a blog post, make a video, draw and post a picture, or attend an event. As with before, you have to get the ball rolling somehow, and there's no better time to start than now, and the best way of putting yourself out onto the advocacy scene is whatever way you're most comfortable with.

Like every other advocate, your platform and audience will start out very small. And that's okay. Remember that starting on a small scale should actually be your initial goal, and that you can have a major impact with even the most limited audience. Depending on what your topic of advocacy is, this might be ideal for you. If you're primarily a self-advocate or if your topic is focused on a smaller-scale issue, then you may never need to reach anybody outside of the circle of people you already know. But after advocating on a smaller (but no less important) scale for a while you may find that you want to expand your reach.

Regarding expanding your audience, I can't promise you

that you'll have the exact same experience as me and wake up one day to find that your platform has exploded online with new people. But at whatever pace it happens, if you continue to be persistent and dedicated and stay true to your message, your platform will also eventually grow, and so should be expanded to accommodate your broader reach.

Growing your platform is exciting and should be celebrated no matter how small that growth is! Making new connections and reaching more people opens up many more opportunities for you to build your platform, share your message, and continue to bring about real change in your community. However, expanding the reach of your advocacy also brings with it new and harder challenges that you will have to face and overcome on your mission to make the world a better place.

But regardless of how large your reach is or how big your platform is, it can be both incredibly hard and incredibly rewarding to be an advocate. That's why in this chapter we'll be breaking down some of the challenges you may encounter as both a new and expanding advocate and how to navigate the turbulence of growing your reach and expanding your potentially community-changing influence.

Safety first

While working as an advocate, one of the most important things to focus on, especially as a young person, is staying safe. Many of the tools you have at your disposal for spreading your message can also put your safety at risk, and so it is of the utmost importance to prioritize your own security above all else. Growing a public-facing advocacy platform to a larger audience will put you at risk for several different safety concerns, and it is important that these are accounted for as you grow your platform and do work as an advocate.

It is worth mentioning that many of the safety tips we'll discuss in this section involve, if you are not already an adult, having a parent or guardian supervise your activities as an advocate so that they could keep you out of harm's way if a dangerous situation were ever to arise. This may very well be the most important thing you can do to protect yourself as a young advocate. This works great if you're lucky enough to have supportive parents (or guardians); however, I do recognize that not everybody is privileged with a family that will be supportive of their advocacy or their message and so may not be willing to help out when it comes to monitoring an advocacy platform.

If this is you, my advice is to put your own safety first. If there aren't trusted adults in your life who are willing to help you stay safe while you advocate, then it is probably best to avoid putting yourself in potentially compromising situations until you are officially an adult. Your large-scale advocacy can wait; the most important thing is keeping yourself safe. And just because you may not have the opportunity to have a public-facing, large-scale advocacy platform right away doesn't mean that you can't advocate to people that you know in person or build your skills as a self-advocate, both of which are less risky than running a large public-facing advocacy platform.

But with that out of the way, let's go over how to stay safe as a young activist in a few different areas.

STAYING SAFE ONLINE

While the hyperconnected internet age that we're living in provides enormous potential for you to spread your ideas far and wide and quickly, if you are not very careful regarding what sort of information you share online and what sort of online activities you take part in you could be putting yourself in a very dangerous situation. Unfortunately, there are many bad people in the world who use the internet to prey on vulnerable people in a variety of ways. Both young people and disabled people are regular targets of internet predators, which means that as young autistic people we are particularly at risk for being victimized. Therefore, it is highly important to practice carefully thought-out internet safety practices.

I tell you this not to scare you or to try to dissuade you from using the internet as part of your advocacy platform, but I'm bringing it up because this is a very serious topic that must not be ignored or taken lightly. Exactly what safety precautions you should take when it comes to internet safety will depend on your specific situation, such as what sorts of activities you plan on partaking in and how old you are, though here we will cover many of the most important things you can do to keep yourself safe online as an advocate.

One of the primary precautions that you should take if you are under the age of 18 is to partner with a parent or trusted guardian to help you set up and manage your online advocacy platform. This becomes more and more important the younger you are, and ideally you should never be running your online social media accounts, website, or public email address by yourself if you are not legally an adult. A trusted parent or guardian has life experience and intuition that you may not have developed yet that they can use to keep your online presence secure and keep you out of the way of potential danger, which may be especially prevalent given that young people on social media are often targeted by predators and other bad people, and this threat does not go away just because an account is for your advocacy work rather than your personal account.

If you are not an adult, it would be most ideal to have a parent or trusted guardian review everything that you intend to post online before you post it. While it is always beneficial to have a means for people to contact you, either through email, a contact form, or social media messaging, it is also most ideal, once again if you are not already an adult, to have a parent or trusted guardian help you read through and respond to any messages you might receive. Both of these recommendations increase in importance the younger you happen to be, and older teen advocates are often capable of managing their own online presence and communications independently, though it's probably better to be on the safe side when it comes to using the internet to promote your advocacy.

And of course, no matter how old you are, there are some general internet safe practices that are always a good idea to follow. Be very careful about what sort of personal information you put out on the internet. Your address, phone number, what school you go to, where you work, and other pieces of personal information that could potentially allow someone to find you in person or contact you through a non-public-facing means should always be kept private. It is amazing how even the tiniest piece of information can allow someone to find out lots of things about you, so it is once again probably best to stay on the side of caution when it comes to what information you post about yourself on the internet.If you can, it may even be worthwhile to run your advocacy platform completely anonymously, especially if you're targeting an audience outside the immediate circle of people who know you personally.

Online security is also very important to help minimize the risk of your accounts and websites becoming compromised. Make sure that you keep all your online accounts safe by choosing strong passwords (containing a variety of numbers, letters, and special characters). If you can, install an anti-malware software on your devices and make regular backups of all your important files. Never open suspicious emails or click on suspicious links, and never put personal information, including email addresses and passwords, into a website you do not absolutely trust.

STAYING SAFE IN PERSON

You may at some point have the opportunity to present about your advocacy at a conference, convention, meeting, or other similar public space. You may also want to attend advocacy functions such as conferences, conventions, and meetings even if you yourself aren't presenting, in addition of course to other in-person advocacy-related events such as protests and meetups. Such activities can be a great way to promote your message, network with other advocates, and ultimately create change. However, just like your online activities, any in-person activity will carry with it a certain amount of risk. As is also the case with advocating online, you are at a greater risk for potential harm as a young person at an in-person advocacy function, with the amount of risk generally increasing the younger you happen to be. It is therefore very important to follow as many safety precautions as possible when attending any in-person advocacy function.

One of the primary ways to keep yourself safe at in-person events is to never go to them alone. 'Safety in numbers' is an adage that has a lot of truth to it, and having another person there provides an enormous safety net to help keep you out of a wide range of dangerous situations. I personally recommend that you always go to any in-person advocacy function with a parent or guardian if you are not yet an adult, and even if you're a young adult it doesn't hurt to go to events with a friend or acquaintance to be extra secure.

Before deciding to attend any event, do some research online about the event, its attendees, and its sponsors. Has this event been held before? If so, what do past attendees say about it? Is it being held at a safe, reputable venue? Who is speaking or presenting at this event, if anybody? What are their credentials? Do their values align ethically with your own? Who is sponsoring this event and are they reputable? Do you agree with the sponsor's values? Asking yourself these questions can help you evaluate the safety of the event in question in addition to ensuring that attending will be beneficial for you.

While attending an advocacy-related event, one of the

best things you can do to boost your advocacy platform and gain allies is to network with fellow advocates. Letting others who are interested in the same sort of advocacy as you are know that your platform exists can open up numerous doors for collaboration and mutual support, both of which will help to boost your message and your influence. However, just like when meeting any stranger for the first time you shouldn't give another advocate you have just met your personal information, even if you recognize their name or their work. It's fine to give the URL of your public-facing website or the handles of your public-facing advocacy-related social media pages, but never give out your phone number, address, the name of your school, or other pieces of private personal information.

You may at some point have the opportunity to present or speak at an in-person event like those we have been discussing. These opportunities can be a challenge for some people for a variety of reasons, though I highly recommend you do your best to take advantage of these opportunities to spread your message and grow your platform. When attending an in-person event as a speaker or presenter the same safety guidelines still apply.

There are however a few more things to keep in mind when it comes to speaking or presenting at events. To begin, you should never be required to pay a fee (beyond standard travel, food, and lodging costs of course, if they are applicable) in order to speak or present at an event. At a bare minimum you should not have to pay anything to the event itself if you are asked to speak or present, and many of the reputable conferences, symposiums, forums, and conventions will pay their speakers for their time or agree to cover travel costs. If you have to pay to speak or give a presentation at an event, then at best the organizers don't care too much about your message and at worst you are getting scammed. It's just not worth it.

This is my recommended minimum set of guidelines, though I have met other advocates who refuse to speak or give a presentation under any circumstance in which they are not paid, and you may wish to adopt a similar policy. After all, going through all the steps of presenting or speaking at an event is hard work, and it's perfectly reasonable to refuse to work without compensation.

STAYING SAFE AT PROTESTS

Few activities embody the spirit of what it means to be an advocate more than the protest. Protesting is a method of influencing social change through a public collective demonstration. Protesting shows both passersby and people in power that there are many people who are displeased with the status quo and are demanding change. Historically speaking, frequent and persistent protesting has been an effective method for influencing societal change. Participating in a protest can be a perfect activity to participate in promoting your cause in your local community.

The vast majority of protests are both peaceful and safe. However, protests can also occasionally turn dangerous, and any time you're in a crowded area with a bunch of strangers you run the same risks that come with attending any in-person event with people you do not know. Safety should therefore be your priority when it comes to participating in a protest.

You should never go to a protest alone. As before, if you are not yet an adult, have a trusted parent, guardian, or other adult come with you. Bring along a friend or two. Stay with another person you know at all times while at a protest. At the very least, tell people where you are going and when you are expecting to leave and come back. Telling people you trust your plans in advance can allow them to quickly take action in the unlikely event that something bad happens to you.

When protesting, I encourage you to be as loud, vocal, and attention-getting as you think is necessary. Make a sign, repeat chants, and generally make you and your group as visible as possible. Standing out is what makes a protest work. However, this must be done both lawfully and safely. Never partake in dangerous or illegal activities, such as lying down in the middle of a road, setting fires, or damaging property. Never attend a protest when you know that others are planning to engage in such actions. You can make a difference and influence change without putting your body in harm's way. If you are at a protest and it looks like things are about to turn violent, the best thing you can do is leave. It doesn't matter if the violence is instigated by other protestors or by outside observers; you do not want to be caught in the crossfire of a dangerous altercation.

The risk of danger at a protest can be mitigated by doing research beforehand. Most protests are pre-organized events, and as with any event you should research the organizers beforehand to get a feel for their philosophy and reputation, along with how safe other protests organized by them have been. The risk of violence can be further mitigated by only protesting during daylight hours and by leaving enough space between you and other people so that you don't get trapped in the middle of a mob should things take a turn for the worse.

Marketing yourself

When it comes to growing your platform, it can often be quite the puzzle to figure out how to transition from advocating to just friends and family to advocating to people from your broader community. Making this jump comes down to marketing yourself, your platform, and your ideas. The action of marketing your advocacy comes down to putting your platform in a position where it can reach more people and then 'selling' those people on your message. Sure, you're probably offering all your content and advocacy work for free in order to better reach people, but marketing principles that are used to sell products and services to more people can also be useful when it comes to reaching more people in order to 'sell' them on your ideas and influence their way of thinking. Marketing is therefore the key way to both grow your platform and convince your audience of your message.

One common expression that is sometimes used to refer to the promotion of something you have created, including your advocacy platform, is 'build it and they'll come.' In other words, so long as you are broadcasting your message out into the world people will naturally start to gather and listen. And as crazy as this sounds, there is a little bit of truth to this simplistic philosophy, all thanks to the internet. From the very beginning of publishing a blog, posting videos on You-Tube, or uploading your thoughts to a social media page, you will receive a small number of views and a small amount of engagement simply from people finding your content through internet search engines and feeds. So long as you continue to produce content with some degree of quality and thoughtfulness your audience and reach will continue to increase, albeit very slowly.

Now, of course, this is not the most efficient way to grow your audience if you desire to do so. Expanding your audience through marketing your platform is an active process, and it does admittedly take a little bit of talent to understand all the ins and outs of how to get noticed. However, there are a few things you can do to give your platform a boost that don't require any specialized knowledge of social trends or internet algorithms.

ENGAGE WITH YOUR AUDIENCE FREQUENTLY

For most intents and purposes, you can think of your advocacy platform as being its own little community. Even if it's just a few people, those out there who have been influenced by and learned something from your work are likely to engage with it through sharing, commenting, and continuing to follow your platform. The key to any thriving community is engagement, and there are several things you can do to increase engagement with your audience.

Always do your best to acknowledge when someone comments virtually on your work. Like or otherwise 'react' to positive comments. Reply to comments frequently and answer as many questions as you can. When you receive legitimate emails or direct messages, do your best to reply to them as well. And, of course, perhaps the best way to keep your audience engaged is by posting frequently. This doesn't mean you have to be burning yourself out by writing extensive essays, or making lengthy videos, or publishing new pieces of art, or producing any other sort of in-depth content. You can keep your audience engaged by posting simple questions, creating polls, sharing short stories (just make sure you aren't giving away any confidential details over the internet!) or writing short posts or tweets about what your advocacy work means to you.

You can also foster engagement for your own platform by engaging with the platforms of other advocates who are fighting for similar things as you. Commenting on other people's work and joining in on social media conversations can help let other people know that you exist and drive more people to your work. Sharing other advocates' work can not only help advance the cause that you believe in, but can also promote interaction and discussion on your own platform. Engaging with other advocates may also eventually lead to opportunities for collaboration, because, after all, nobody can change the world alone.

ACTIVELY SEARCH FOR OPPORTUNITIES

While it's fun to think about there one day being a time where opportunities to spread your message will come knocking on your door without you having to do anything, in the real world you will generally have to do a bit of active searching if you want to find chances to give presentations, make speeches, or meet with influential people. Sometimes you can find opportunities to advocate with a quick internet search. Look online to find upcoming conferences and symposiums in your area which are relevant to your topic and are looking for speakers or presenters. If you find one that you would be interested in presenting at and you meet the criteria, go ahead and submit an application (with your parent's or guardian's permission if you are not yet an adult, of course). The worst that can happen is that you'll be turned down, in which case you can apply next year or try somewhere else.

Another good way to find opportunities to share your message and ideas is to engage with and follow fellow advocates. Following what fellow advocates have been up to can give you ideas about where you might want to focus your efforts in the future. For example, if an advocate you admire has given a speech at a particular symposium, then perhaps that event is somewhere you could try to present at in the future.

Finally, it never hurts to reach out to people and ask if they can help you promote your platform. Ask fellow advocates if you can write a guest post on their blog. Ask a teacher if you can give a quick presentation to your class one day. Ask a friend or family member to give a tip to the local newspaper about the advocacy work you're doing in your community. There may be many opportunities near to you and ready for you to take advantage of. All you need to do is ask.

ASK FRIENDS AND FAMILY TO SHARE YOUR WORK

Finally, it's never a bad idea to simply ask people in your life who care about you to share your work with other people. Generally, your friends and close family will be more than happy to tell their acquaintances about your platform or share your work to their social media pages, and this can be a fantastic way for your ideas to gain just a little bit more exposure, especially when your platform is still relatively small.

Understanding algorithms and analytics

By doing your best to follow the tips we just talked about, you can make your platform much more appealing and visible to a potential audience, allowing you to spread greater awareness of your topic. These relatively simple strategies require very little specialized knowledge, though of course they are not the be-all and end-all when it comes to promoting your platform and growing your audience. In today's hyperconnected world, most of the major growth in attention that your platform will experience will be due to the internet, even if all your work is being done locally.

Therefore, let's next talk a little bit about the art and science of optimizing your online platform to reach as many people as possible. Before we go on though, I want to point out that this is a very complex topic, and we will barely be scratching the surface here. I also want you to remember that you don't need to have a massive online presence, or any online presence at all for that matter, to be a good advocate. Your goal is to make the world a better place, not to accumulate as many followers as you can, and it is certainly possible to do one without the other.

The internet is perhaps the single most mysterious thing that humans have ever invented. It drives our collective culture and consciousness, which can be a great thing when you're trying to use it to influence people's outlook on specific issues, but it does so in a manner that can at times be completely unpredictable. Whenever your content on an online platform, whether it be your blog, YouTube channel, or social media post, is seen by someone else it is due to a complex set of algorithms. Algorithms in this context refer to the programming used by the website to figure out whether or not, or to what degree, a piece of content is shown to its userbase. When you scroll through a social media feed the posts, pictures, and videos that you see are being shown to you are there because they were selected by the website's algorithms to show up in your feed or be recommended to you.

It makes sense then that if you want your internet content to be discoverable by more people you should design it so that it is more likely to appear in more people's feeds. In my experience, social media algorithms tend to favor content that is engaging: content which gets more likes, comments, and shares. The more engagement a post receives, the greater its reach tends to be. Techniques for making your posts more engaging, such as posting more frequently and engaging with your audience in the comments, can be a great way to expand your platform's social media reach.

You can increase engagement even further by taking into consideration the demographics and analytics of your followers. Demographics refers to the particular makeup of your followers: what ages they are, where they live, what they are interested in, and other bits of data and information about them. Analytics refers to analyzing patterns around how your followers engage with your work, such as what times of the day and week your posts are most popular and what sorts of content your audience enjoys. The demographics and analytics of your platform can be either very straightforward or very complicated depending on factors such as how wide-reaching your advocacy work is and how broad your topic is. It is also likely that the demographics of your audience will be different across different internet sites. Facebook tends to draw a very different audience than Twitter or Instagram, and patterns such as these will be reflected in the followers of your platform on various sites.

But with a little bit of strategic thinking it is possible to custom-tailor what, when, and how you post in order to maximize the amount of engagement your platform gets, and in return how widely seen your message is. After a little while of promoting your message via social media, you may start to notice patterns in how your posts are received by your audience. Maybe you get more likes, shares, and comments at certain times of the day. Maybe different types of content tend to be received better. Whatever it is, do your best to use these patterns to your advantage, posting at times when engagement is highest and formatting your message in a way that people seem to enjoy. It might also be worth figuring out where in the world your followers tend to be from and what parts of your message might be most impactful to them based on their circumstances and cater your posting accordingly to maximize the relevance, and therefore the effectiveness, of your message and the reach of your platform.

Being able to understand the demographics and analytics

of your audience and using that knowledge to make strategic decisions about your posting is a skill that must be developed over time with practice and experience, and there is much more to this practice than can be addressed in just one section. But just as with anything, you have to start somewhere, and just a little bit of thought put into the demographic makeup of your platform's followers can have a big payoff when it comes to boosting the social media reach of your platform, and therefore expanding the impact of your advocacy work.

Telling stories

Storytelling has been an important part of human culture for a very long time. Ever since our stone age ancestors used to huddle around the fire and relay tales of the day's hunt, our brains have been primed to engage with and care about stories. You can use this to your advantage to make your platform more engaging for your audience and as a result maximize the impact that your influence will have in the real world.

Storytelling should weave throughout your platform in both straightforward and less obvious ways. Right up front, telling a story about why your topic of advocacy is important to you is not only a good way to increase the engagement of your audience but also helps people to understand the relevance of what you are advocating for. This can help persuade people, including people with a great deal of influence such as politicians, to become motivated to take action. Storytelling can do this in a way that simply citing raw statistics cannot. People like stories; we are biologically programmed to engage with stories and empathize with the characters within them. When you frame your topic through a story it suddenly becomes real and relevant to the people who are listening, and as such your advocacy will be more impactful.

If you want to truly give your platform an engagement boost, though, you should aim to incorporate storytelling into every facet of your message. However, don't be mistaken: this doesn't necessarily mean that you have to be retelling or making up stories all the time. You see, what really defines a story is not so much its content as its structure. Stories have distinct beginning, middle, and ending sections. They feature a conflict that must be resolved or overcome by the characters before a final resolution is brought forth.

Every story follows a very specific pattern: there is a beginning in which the main characters are introduced and the status quo is interrupted by some sort of conflict. The word conflict may conjure up images of intense feuds and emotional struggle, and indeed in some stories this may be the case, but in this context the 'conflict' is simply any event that disrupts the status quo established in the beginning. There is then the longest part of the story, the middle or 'rising action,' in which the main characters engage with (and very often struggle with) the conflict that the plot of the story is based around. The middle section usually ends with a climax, where interaction between the characters and the conflict is at its greatest and most important. Finally, there is the ending, where the characters resolve the story's conflict and return to a new sense of normal. This structure is sometimes called the 'hero arc,' and just about every story that is told, from an epic saga such as *The Lord of the Rings* all the way to a simple true story about that one time you saw a fox while walking home from the grocery store, can be broken down according to this arc.

As an example of how you can use storytelling to make your platform more engaging, think back to the previous chapter where we talked very briefly about how your message should follow a sort of story arc. Calling out changes that need to occur corresponds roughly with the beginning section of a story. You're identifying the conflict and the affected characters while highlighting the importance of your topic by contrasting the status quo (how things are) with how things should be. By suggesting actions that need to be taken, in addition to educating others on the best course of action, you are also creating a sort of rising action. You are helping people to mentally work through the conflict at hand, all the while drawing them in closer and getting them to care about the issue. And of course, looking forward to the future corresponds to the end and resolution of the story. However, in the case of your advocacy message the resolution is something that has not yet happened (if we were already there you would have no reason to be advocating). Where this leaves your audience then is right in the middle of the climax. You are telling your listeners that the conflict has come to a head and that it is time to take action and that they're the ones who can make it happen.

This is why this way of framing your message is such an effective way of calling out the issues in your community you are hoping to address. It motivates people to change their thinking and their behavior, which is what ultimately results in real change. In this way, the ancient art of storytelling can be used to make your platform both more engaging, and therefore more likely to attract more followers, and more effective at impacting your community for the better.

Self-care

Being an advocate is hard work, and it is an activity that can and very often will take a toll on your mental health. That's simply the reality of it; I have no intention of taking the advocacy experience and dipping it in chocolate, covering it in strawberry syrup, and then packaging it all up with a nice little red bow on top. This is one of the main reasons why, as we have previously discussed, it is so important that you are deeply invested in your topic and that you let your passion for seeing change in your community drive you past the obstacles that you will face.

For your own sake, however, it is very important that you have a toolkit of strategies that you can use to manage your own mental health, both within the context of advocacy work and in other places in your life. Anxiety, depression, and other mental health conditions are unfortunately very prevalent in the autistic population, and if you're not careful partaking in advocacy activities can very often make these worse. Everybody's needs are a little bit different, and so there is no one-size-fits-all approach to managing mental health. What I hope to give you though is a set of strategies that you might use to keep your mental health in check when faced with various scenarios you may encounter as an advocate. But ultimately you should do what works best for you. Don't be afraid to use tools and techniques that you've developed yourself or learned from other sources if they make you feel better.

Spoon Theory

When it comes to talking about mental health, self-care, and energy expenditure, I always like to employ a metaphor which is commonly used within various disability communities, including the autistic community, known as Spoon Theory. Spoon Theory was originally developed by Christine Miserandino to describe what it's like to live with an autoimmune disease called lupus;[1] however, the metaphor can be useful for just about anyone.

Within Spoon Theory, a 'spoon' is a unit, specifically a unit of emotional, mental, and/or physical energy that a person possesses in that particular moment. Each day we have a certain number of spoons that we can expend in order to do certain activities or complete certain tasks. For example, braving sensory overload by entering a crowded grocery store takes away a certain number of spoons that cannot be used on something else. Some people start off each day with more than enough spoons to make it through the day without any thought, but other people, especially us neurodivergent people, may not have as many spoons available every day and doing the same activities may require that we use more spoons,

---

1   Miserandino, Christine. 'The Spoon Theory.' But You Don't Look Sick. https://butyoudontlooksick.com/articles/written-by-christine/the-spoon-theory

which means we must carefully ration our spoons to avoid burning out or shutting down.

Let's say that a hypothetical person starts their day with ten spoons. During that day, they need to get themselves ready in the morning, go to the corner shop for snacks, and work on homework. Getting ready may require that this person expend two spoons, going to the shop takes three spoons, and working on homework takes four spoons. By the end of the day they only have one spoon left, and so are probably feeling pretty exhausted and don't have the energy left to do any more major tasks in the evening. If they had something planned for that evening, then they would have to drop another activity earlier in the day to accommodate the extra spoon loss.

We all start each day with a different number of spoons, and different activities will require differing numbers of spoons for different people due to differences in the way that we're wired. For the same reason, we all replenish spoons at a different rate. Some people may be able to recover all their spoons over a single full night's rest; others may take weeks to regain all their lost spoons. But whatever your spoon situation happens to be, the likelihood is that you're going to have to think about how to ration your spoons, especially when you become active as an advocate.

Spoon Theory forms a large part of the base for managing your mental health as an advocate and avoiding burnout. You don't have to assign a specific number to how many spoons you have or how many spoons you'll lose by doing a certain thing, but it is important to always be thinking generally about how many spoons you'll need to expend in a certain day so that you can space out activities and give yourself time to rest and recover, which may very well be the basis for managing your mental health as an autistic advocate.

If you ever feel like you're running low on spoons, becoming overwhelmed, or getting close to burnout, the best thing you can do is simply step back, take a break, and come back later. Your advocacy is important, but your own personal mental health is even more important. Taking care of yourself is important for both your own personal well-being and the effectiveness of your advocacy. Take a step back and focus on a special interest or an activity that you enjoy to let yourself decompress. Take some time to manage your sensory and emotional input, avoiding environments that overwhelm you and content that upsets you. You don't owe the world anything, and you are not obligated to advocate at every moment of every day if it's harming your mental, emotional, or physical well-being.

Dealing with criticism

While seeing the results of advocacy and outreach can be pretty thrilling, there's also a downside that I feel necessary to share with you. When you open yourself up to the world and give complete strangers a glimpse into some of the most intimate details of your life while exposing your vulnerabilities, you won't always be met with love, hugs, and accolades. In fact, sometimes the response can be downright mean and even downright scary.

One of the major challenges that comes with being an advocate is that no matter what your message is, you're bound to attract nay-sayers, haters, bullies, trolls, and other such people who will be anything but supportive of your message. This is especially true if your platform has an internet presence. Unfortunately, the response that many people have to hearing someone express an idea with which they disagree or are ideologically opposed to is for them to become very angry and aggressive, occasionally going to great lengths in an attempt to hurt the person with whom they disagree. It is important if and when such a scenario arises that you know how to handle the situation and your own mental health at the same time.

One hard truth that starts to really sink in as you participate more and more in advocacy work is that you will not convince everybody that what you believe in is correct. No matter how good your arguments are, no matter how well you communicate your message, and no matter how much better you want to make the world there will always be some people, chances are a lot of people, who will never go along with your ideas or want to make the changes you are proposing.

Fortunately, not everybody who disagrees with you will be mean or disrespectful about it and the people who would then go out of their way to harass you are an even smaller minority. However, whenever you face resistance to your advocacy, whether online, in-person, from someone you know personally, or a complete stranger, you have to always be thinking about whether it is worth the time and lost spoons to try to debate, discuss, or argue with a detractor.

Sometimes this is a fairly easy decision to make. In my experience, if someone is engaging in bullying you, harassing you, being disrespectful to you, or is just generally being unpleasant it is almost never worth the time to try to engage with them. Block them. Don't reply to them. Walk away. Don't waste any time thinking about or engaging with them, and don't let their negativity into your life. You will be much happier if you simply ignore the people who are criticizing you and, to use a common internet phrase, 'don't feed the trolls.' I know it can be hard to back down when your ideas are being challenged, but when someone is being hostile they are almost always more trouble than they're worth. Your spoons are better spent, and will have a bigger impact, elsewhere. You're the author of your own story, not the people who criticize you.

Other times it is more difficult to tell whether or not to engage. Some people will have the decency to be respectful when disagreeing publicly with your ideas or your platform. These types of interactions are always much more pleasant when compared to hostile critics who will drain away your emotional spoons very quickly and have the potential to leave your self-esteem in tatters. In these cases, it may be worth it to engage in dialogue and debate with these critics. You're still very unlikely to convince them of anything - if they're going to take the time to make a comment to you then they're probably fairly deep set into their position - but when you debate with someone in a public setting your ultimate goal is not to change your opponent's mind, but rather to change your audience's mind. Refuting a challenge to your platform or ideas can go a long way in showing observers that your proposals and calls for change have merit, in addition to limiting the negative impact that criticism may have.

Of course, this only works if you're being challenged somewhere that is at least semi-public. If you receive a negative email, for example, it's probably not worth it to respond even if the person who sent the email isn't being a bully because there will be no outside observers who might be persuaded by your refutation. All in all, the decision about whether to respond to criticism comes down to several factors, such as the tone of the dialogue, the number of spoons you have, and the publicity of the venue, and these decisions must be made on a case-by-case basis. Hopefully I have given you some things to think about to help guide you through this decision-making process.

When facing criticism, one of the most important things you can have to keep your self-esteem up and prevent yourself from being overwhelmed is a strong community and support network who can encourage you and affirm your vision as an advocate. If you're lucky enough to have parents or guardians who are supportive of your work, then they can act as a very strong emotional support to keep you grounded when facing criticism. Friends can also be a fantastic source of encouragement as can an online community of other advocates in your field. Wherever this sort of support is coming from, it is critical to have people in your life in some sense who are on your side and who believe in your mission.

Finally, another protective measure you may want to take is to have a trusted person, such as a parent or guardian, pre-screen comments and emails sent to you to protect you from any harassment. A trusted person can delete any abusive communication sent to you before you are able to see it and be affected by it, which can save you a lot of stress in the long run, not to mention that this pre-screening strategy can be a good general internet safety measure as well. Some online blogging sites such as Wordpress allow you to turn on something called 'comment approval,' where somebody has to approve comments before they are publicly visible, which can be a good tool to use to prevent trolls and other negative people from leaving strings of inappropriate comments on your site.

And of course, hearing respectful criticism of your opinions can help you better understand and refine your arguments, or perhaps even refine your own thinking on issues that are important to you and your community. You don't have to be scared of criticism. If your ideas are good then they should stand for themselves. Criticism can also be used as a form of motivation to help you get out there and prove your critics wrong.

Managing disappointment

One of the few things that I can guarantee you about what it's like to be an advocate is that you will be faced with a great deal of disappointment, probably multiple times over. It sort of comes with the job. Though I do believe that you will generally find advocacy to be a very rewarding way to spend your time if you are passionate about your topic, not everything is going to go the way that you want or expect, so disappointment is an emotion that you'll come across quite frequently as well. In whatever form it takes, it is important to know how to manage disappointment when we feel it.

Because we're autistic, we generally tend to feel emotions more strongly, and this of course includes disappointment. This makes it doubly difficult for us when we experience it. This may not work for everybody, but I have found that it can sometimes be helpful to acknowledge to yourself that you're feeling disappointed. What happened didn't go your way, and you don't have to pretend that everything is alright. It is perfectly acceptable, and expected, that you will encounter disappointment while advocating for what you believe in. Acknowledge that what you're feeling is real and valid, and that it is okay to feel that way. Recognizing and acknowledging that your feelings are appropriate can sometimes make you feel a little bit better, especially if you're like me and you have a tendency to feel anxious or guilty about feeling your negative feelings. It is perfectly fine and expected to feel disappointed or downtrodden sometimes. If you need to, write this down or say it to yourself out loud or in your head whenever you start to get anxious about your feelings.

Another thing to recognize when something doesn't go quite the way you would have liked is that your best, whatever your best is, is always good enough. What this means is that you don't have to hold yourself to someone else's standard of success; the most that you can ever do is your best, and everyone's best will look a little bit different. So as long as you have done your best, no matter what the results are, then you have done everything that you could do and therefore there is no reason to be hard on yourself.

Of course, as you may very well be familiar with, strong emotions don't exactly respond to logical thinking and so it's definitely possible to feel very strongly disappointed in yourself if something doesn't go the way you wanted it to. But thinking in terms of doing your best rather than thinking in terms of getting a specific result can be very helpful for your mental health overall. Whenever you feel yourself getting anxious or upset at yourself over not getting a desired result, remember, and repeat to yourself if necessary, that you did your best and that your best is enough.

Finally, when you're facing disappointment it is often helpful to look forward to future opportunities rather than dwell on what didn't go as you expected. This is another concept that is very simple in theory but can be very complicated in practice. My brain tends to run in circles when I'm upset about something: I focus in on what's causing me stress and I literally can't think about or focus on anything else. This seems to be pretty common in autistic people - perhaps you can relate. This fact makes it difficult to look to the future instead of focusing on the past.

What has helped me break this cycle in the past has been a visual aid, specifically a list. Write or type out a list of things you want to try to advance your platform, whether it be applying for speaking opportunities, starting a petition, organizing a protest, and so on. Once you have a sizeable list, if one opportunity doesn't go as you would like you can simply cross it off the list and move on to the next item. This can help to prevent your brain from obsessing over one missed opportunity because you can simply cross it off the list and move on to whatever is next. It allows you to see each opportunity as but one of many, which can be very helpful in overcoming disappointment that may come from an unsuccessful attempt at advocacy.

In the end though, as individuals we all have different ways of handling disappointment and other strong emotions, and so different techniques, including many that have not been listed here, will work for different people. The most important part is to recognize that facing disappointment is an inevitable part of being an advocate and to have a plan for how you are going to manage disappointment in order to preserve your own mental health and well-being.

Concluding thoughts

Putting yourself, your story, and your ideas out there into the world can carry with it a range of different emotions, from the tingling energy that comes from the excitement of seeing your work make an impact, to the tediousness of getting your work noticed, to the overwhelming onslaught of social media obligations. Growing your platform is often a slow process that brings with it both increasing complexity and an increasing opportunity to make change, and with these heightened opportunities and responsibilities thinking about personal safety, marketing, and self-care is a must.

In the next chapter, we'll take a look at troubleshooting several potential obstacles that you may run into as an advocate as we discuss defeating labels and stereotypes, reaching out to other people, plagiarism and how to avoid it, recognizing logical fallacies, and staying persistent.

Interview 5:
Madi on advocacy and managing mental health

Putting yourself out there and growing your platform are complex topics that require a certain amount of experience to fully implement. This is why our next interview is with 18-year-old Madi Kenna from Queensland, Australia. Madi is an autism and LGBTQ+ advocate, providing a poignant and much-needed perspective on these topics and their intersectionality as someone who is both queer and autistic. Madi has served on the YMCA Queensland Youth Parliament on the Committee for Health and Disability Services since 2019 and has also worked for the I CAN Network as a peer mentor. Here are Madi's answers to questions regarding putting yourself out there as a young, autistic advocate:

You've talked before about how you've struggled with your identity in the past. How has engaging as an advocate and being part of an advocacy community helped you to better understand and come to terms with yourself?

I have always been open about being autistic. Even when other people have presumed things about me, I have always wanted to educate others about autism. When people see that someone who 'doesn't look autistic' say they have autism, their mind is automatically opened to the possibility of autism being something more than what they previously thought. But this wasn't enough for me. I started learning more about autism to be able to educate others even more. From this, I started to learn more about myself and *my* autism.

I have only been able to become this confident in my identity because of how I was introduced to autism. We first started understanding my autism after watching Temple Grandin. I related to many of her traits and symptoms. I am so grateful to have a role model who is so openly proud and confident to shape my idea of autism. Everyone deserves a role model and I hope to be that for others.

Have you found that your advocacy platform tends to grow in size on its own or do you find you have to actively promote your work to grow your audience? If you find yourself actively promoting your work, what methods have you found to be the most useful for reaching a wider audience?

When I found Queensland Youth Parliament, a youth program with The Y in Australia to promote young voices, it gave me a platform like no other. I have always valued small changes. Something as little as calling out offensive comments about autism in the playground can change someone's perspective forever. At first, I only challenged people around me who spoke negatively about autism. As time passed on, I realized this wasn't enough for me. I knew I needed to find a platform of my own to share my story. I started finding more interest in autism advocates. I started attending autism workshops and speaking to other people who were passionate about autism like me. Networking is a crucial part in growing my platform and finding my voice as an autistic advocate.

Like many advocates, I'm sure you've had to face a fair amount of criticism in the past. How have you handled criticism, and what have you found to be helpful for maintaining your high sense of self-esteem when you've faced criticism?

Most criticism I have received has questioned my identity and whether or not I even have autism. Otherwise just completely dismissing the challenges of autism by saying, 'Well, everyone is a little bit autistic.' This led me to question my identity too. There are times when I allow the stigmas and toxic thoughts of others to impact my well-being. I have a strong support network around me - my family and my psychologist play a massive role in my life. Over the years, through one-on-one psychology sessions and various group programs, I have developed a toolbox containing all the ways I can understand situations, regulate my emotions, and to process circumstances that may be confronting or confusing. When it comes to direct criticism, I write down parts of my identity I know are true to remind me of my values and morals. This helps me move closer to the best Madi I can be.

Advocacy work can definitely take a lot of time and energy. How have you been able to balance your advocacy activities with the rest of your personal life, and how have you been able to pace yourself so that you don't burn yourself out while fighting to make change in your community?

Professor Tony Attwood and Dr Michelle Garnett introduced me to the concept of 'energy accounting' and it changed the way I look at a work-life balance forever. I ask the questions, 'Does this activity give me energy or take away energy?' and 'How much energy does it give/take away?' For example, going to a camp could take away 60 percent of my energy, but watching *Doctor Who* and drawing gives back 30 percent of that energy. I then put these into columns of either 'deposit energy' or 'withdraw energy' and how much energy it gives/ takes. This helps me understand how I can recover from tiring situations or 'withdrawals.' We also discovered that 'withdrawals' aren't always bad or negative experiences. That camp, for example, was one of the best experiences of my life, but if I don't 'deposit' energy I can't recover properly. We can't cut out every 'withdrawal,' but we can 'deposit' energy to compensate. My support network is also very important here. We like to use the analogy of a tennis player. Although I am out on the court on my own, I couldn't have gotten there without my team, through training and preparation. They are always there to support me, and I am so grateful for them.

If you can think of one, what was your scariest moment as an advocate, and how did you manage to safely handle the situation?

The scariest moments are always before something big happens, because I don't know for certain what is going to happen. For example, giving a speech or meeting new people. I think of anything and everything that could go wrong (none of which have ever actually happened). I have such a strong team around me to help me stay calm and rationalize the situation. All I have to do is ask for help, as scary as that can seem sometimes.

What advice, if any, would you give to an aspiring young autistic advocate who wants to make change in the world?

It can be difficult to know where to start, but don't put pressure on yourself to impact the whole world overnight. Break down your goals and start small. Even if that is just correcting someone talking ill of autism. That can change someone's whole life. Take initiative and seek out opportunities; don't wait for them to come to you. Every person you interact with has then had an experience with autism. Telling your story and sharing your experiences as an autistic individual is so powerful. And as Temple Grandin said, we are 'different, not less.'

Madi can be found online at the following:
Facebook: Madi Kenna - Autism Advocate[2]
On the web: www.madikenna.com

---

2   www.facebook.com/MJKautism

CHAPTER 6

Troubleshooting for the Everyday Autistic Advocate

One of my favorite quotes of all time comes from a 1937 issue of *Astronautics* magazine, where it is proclaimed that 'A good rule for rocket experimenters to follow is this: always assume that it will explode.'[1] You have to admit, it's a pretty funny quote. The deadpan acknowledgement of the total and utter failure that is bound to come with the field may seem to be humorously unusual for an enthusiast's magazine, but there's actually a lot of wisdom in it. By expecting the unexpected, expecting that something along the way is bound to go wrong, you can better prepare yourself when there are bumps in the road.

Being an advocate means going on a journey that is a virtual minefield of ups and downs. Failure is just as common, if not more common, than success for advocates and activists. This is a pretty key thing to take away from this book, if you haven't already. Expecting the bumpy road ahead and

---

1   'Letters to the Editor.' *Astronautics Magazine*. 1937, p. 8. https://arc.aiaa.org/toc/jastn/7/38

the obstacles and setbacks you may run into will help you be better prepared for when the going gets tough.

We've already explored several problems that may come up and how to deal with them. So far we've covered building self-confidence, overcoming executive dysfunction to start up an advocacy platform, fighting through the communication slog, staying safe, and protecting your mental health while dealing with criticism and online bullying, among other things. However, if there's one thing I've learned from the time I've spent as an advocate it's that there are countless ways that something can go wrong, so it is important to have strategies in place to work through the challenges.

This final chapter will be dedicated to going over a few more tips and bits of information that you may find useful. Think of it as 'debugging' your platform, allowing you to be aware of and know how to handle a few more of the potential obstacles as they come up so you can pass them more easily.

Now obviously, I do not own a crystal ball. I cannot foresee every possible challenge and obstacle that you may face while doing advocacy and activism, but ahead lie solutions to some of the more common problems facing autistic advocates: stereotyping, starting conversations, plagiarism and copyright, logical fallacies, and staying persistent even when no change seems to be occurring.

Defeating labels and stereotypes

It's my opinion that one of the most frustrating parts about being autistic is dealing with many of the untrue stereotypes that people have about what autism is, what autistic people are like, and what we are capable of. In this context, a stereotype is a broad, generally incorrect generalization that is applied to a person or group of people by others based on their own prejudices or limited experience, and stereotypes abound when it comes to autism and autistic people.

Stereotypes are frustrating because they can often limit the opportunities that are made available to us. Stereotypes may make people assume things about you which are not true, which is why being able to defeat them is an important part of being an advocate. Stereotypes exist for all sorts of different demographics of people, not just autistic people, but here let's focus specifically on stereotypes relating to autism and autistic people, with the following advice being based on what has worked for me in the past.

Perhaps the most straightforward way to combat stereotypes of just about any type is to simply be true to yourself. If other people have an idea about you that is false, prove them wrong. Many people hold stereotypes about autistic people unintentionally simply because they don't understand autism very well, so by simply showing them how their preconceived notions are wrong you can help correct their perceptions and reduce future stereotyping for both yourself and others. For example, it is a common stereotype that autistic people are always unathletic. Though this might be true for some people, if you enjoy physical activity or playing sports then don't be afraid to mention that as part of your identity. Challenge stereotypes head on by being your authentic self rather than trying to conform to other people's expectations of what you should be like.

Other people are more stuck in their ways with their stereotyping. It's not uncommon for autistic people who don't fit someone else's expectations of what autistic people are supposed to be like to be accused of faking being autistic. This is especially true if your topic of advocacy just so happens to be related to autism and neurodiversity, because appealing to existing stereotypes is a convenient way for detractors to attempt to shut you out of the conversation. Other people simply can't see past their own prejudices and will always fail to comprehend how stereotypes may not apply to you. For people such as these, it may once again be worth asking yourself whether it is even worth engaging with them at all. Your energy is probably better spent elsewhere on people who are willing to open their minds and see past their preconceptions of you in order to listen to your message.

I would also like to point out one specific type of stereotyping that is very commonly applied towards autistic people: attempts to pigeonhole us into specific arbitrary categories. The most prevalent of this type of stereotyping is through the use of functioning labels. You've probably heard functioning labels being used before: 'so-and-so has "high functioning" autism' or alternatively 'my sister is a "low functioning" autistic.' Functioning labels can also take the form of labeling someone either 'mildly' or 'severely' autistic, or through phrases such as, 'You're only a little bit autistic.' Maybe you've even used terminology in the past to refer to yourself or others because this is what you have heard used by other people.

However, functioning labels might be some of the most prevalent and harmful form of stereotyping for autistic

advocates, particularly autistic advocates doing autism advocacy. Allow me to explain how and why. Autism is referred
to as being a spectrum, which means that no two of us are
exactly alike. But the autism spectrum is not linear. It is not
a one-dimensional spectrum labeled 'mild' on one end and
'severe' on the other; just because you excel in one area does
not mean that you don't need significant support in another
area, and vice versa. This makes it just about impossible to
accurately label anybody as being any sort of functioning
without making sweeping generalizations. Autism is simply
far more complicated than simple functioning labels make it
out to be.

Functioning labels are also arbitrary in the sense that
there is no one set definition of what is low or high functioning or what is mild or severe. The leads to many of us being
labeled 'high functioning' by some people or at one point in
our lives and 'low functioning' by other people or at different
points in our lives. You could probably make a case that just
about any autistic person could be seen as both high and low
functioning at the same time depending on what character-
istics are focused on.

Functioning labels fall into the category of stereotyping
not only because of their broad-brushing and often inaccu-
rate nature, but also because they can often be very harmful.
If someone is labeled as high functioning, people may assume
they don't need any supports, while if someone is labeled
low functioning people may assume that they are incapable
of doing anything. Both situations are detrimental. If you go
into autism and neurodiversity advocacy, you will probably
also see functioning label stereotypes weaponized by people

who oppose your message. It is common for autistic advocates, including those with many challenges and high support
needs, to be told by critics that they are 'too high functioning'
to be able to be worthy as an autism advocate.

Countering functioning label stereotypes is a communi-
ty-wide process that you can help take part in. Functioning
labels, despite their flaws, are pervasive when the topic of
autism comes up, and most people use them simply because
they have heard other people use them or it's all they know
when it comes to communicating about someone's support
needs. The key here, similar in fashion to countering other
stereotypes, is education. It is important to call out functioning labels, particularly functioning labels that are being used
in a harmful way or for stereotyping, when you see them and
bring to attention the trouble with them and the harm they
can potentially cause.

But of perhaps even greater importance than this is to
provide alternatives for people to use in place of functioning labels. Many people who use functioning labels do so
because they are trying to communicate information about
a particular person's support needs, and they may not know
how to do this without using functioning labels. By providing
an alternative, you can help people communicate without
unintentionally stereotyping. What I typically tell people
who are looking for an alternative to functioning labels is to
be specific when discussing their own or somebody else's
needs rather than trying to rely on a catch-all label to do that
for them. Tell people that rather than simply saying low or
high functioning, they should specify what a person's needs,
strengths, and challenges are. It takes a little bit more work,

but it will be far more practically helpful than an overgeneralized and potentially harmful label.

Defeating stereotypes means facing them head on and running straight through them. People hold to stereotypes because of (often unconscious) prejudices they carry about a group of people or simply because of a lack of experience, and often the best form of education in these cases is a demonstration. By being your authentic self, you can help bust stereotypes both now and in the future, influencing just one person at a time to see the bigger picture. And in the meantime, keep pushing forward and focus your efforts on those who will see you for who you really are, not for what they think you should be.

How to talk to humans

Advocacy is by definition a social activity. Advocacy involves tackling social problems head on, steering societal change through activism, and inspiring others to do the same. Advocacy ultimately revolves around reaching out to others to assert yourself, asking for help, and generally communicating your message in order to create waves of change through your community. Reaching out to teachers or employers about accommodations that you will need is an important part of self-advocacy, while organizing and attending events, networking with fellow advocates, writing to legislators, and countless other advocacy activities involve being able to initiate a conversation, even if in writing, with another person.

Here's the thing though: talking to people is hard. Like,

really hard. Humans are often highly confusing and illogical, and it can sometimes be hard to know what to say or how to start a conversation. Additionally, I find that sometimes I will know what I want to say in my head, but I don't know what words to use to articulate it, and as you know if you experience the same, this can make talking to other people almost impossible.

Something that's often recommended to help with knowing what to say is to follow a script, so that you know beforehand what you're going to say or how you're going to open a conversation. While this can occasionally be helpful, scripts have the problem of not being very flexible in real-world scenarios and it's hard to craft a script for every specific scenario you may encounter. What is preferable to scripts then is a framework that can be used as a sort of guide to reaching out to people. I have found one such framework that I think is very useful, and I want to tell you about it here. It is called the 'Inigo Montoya Method.'[2]

To get a grasp of what this method is all about, first we must talk about movies, specifically the 1987 film *The Princess Bride*. Without digging too deep into specific plot points, there is a very famous scene in the movie where the hero of the story, Inigo Montoya, confronts his nemesis during a sword fight with the phrase 'My name is Inigo Montoya. You killed my father. Prepare to die.'[3] It's a short and quippy

---

2   Wayne, Rachel. 'Networking 101: The Inigo Montoya Method.' Medium. 2020. https://medium.com/the-post-grad-survival-guide/networking-101-the-inigo-montoya-method-76a69a617d69

3   *The Princess Bride*. Directed by Rob Reiner. 1987.

phrase that's easy to remember and can be used as a guide for how to start conversations that have a purpose.

According to the Inigo Montoya Method, each of Inigo's three sentences in that phrase can be seen as generalizations for three steps to initiate a conversation: introduce yourself, give a relevant personal link, and then lay out your expectations. You can use these three steps any time you need to start a conversation with or reach out to someone that you aren't super well acquainted with. It may not be the way to talk to your friends all the time, but it is perfect for writing and responding to emails, messages, comments, and while networking. Let's break down each of these three steps and work through some examples of how you can use them when you need to reach out to other people as an advocate.

Step 1: Introduce yourself – 'My name is Inigo Montoya.' Following the lead of Montoya, the first thing you should do when addressing someone, especially someone you've never met before, is to introduce yourself with your name. This can be as simple as saying 'My name is...'; however, it is also generally advisable to start with a simple greeting by starting with something such as 'Hello, my name is...'.

This step is very straightforward if you are writing to someone; however, if you are talking to someone in person it can become slightly more complicated. If you are speaking with someone in person, after you introduce yourself it is common for the other person to then introduce themself to you (even if you know who they are). If you already know the person you are talking with you don't necessarily have to tell them your name again, but an introduction of some kind is still useful for opening the conversation. A simple opening such as 'I have a proposal for you,' or 'I need your help,' or 'We need to talk about something' is all that is needed to open the conversation.

Step 2: Give a relevant personal link – 'You killed my father.' What Inigo does next is connect himself to his purpose: why he is there and why he is having the conversation. Providing a personal link need not be complicated. In fact, it may be possible to combine your introduction and personal link into one sentence. A personal link is any detail that connects you, the person you are writing or speaking to, and the issue at hand in a way that provides context for your conversation. Your personal link could be just about anything and will vary greatly from situation to situation.

If you're writing to someone from your school about accommodations you might mention that you are a student. If you're networking with a fellow advocate, you might mention that you've done similar work to them and are interested in the same things. If you're writing to a legislator, you might mention that you live in the region represented by said legislator. You could also try writing a little bit about why you're passionate about your topic of advocacy or how it affects you as a person. Anything that gives context for why you are starting the conversation will work.

Step 3: Manage expectations – 'Prepare to die.' The last step in the Montoya Method is the part where you lay down exactly what you came to talk (or write) about. After you have moved past the pleasantries of introducing yourself and providing context for your request, question, or concern, it's now time to get down to business. Articulate what it is that you expect from the other person; don't be afraid to say what you mean or ask for what you need, and be blunt if necessary. This portion of your conversation can generally be scripted out beforehand if you are speaking in person and have trouble with spontaneous speech.

And there you have it. In just three steps you've initiated a conversation and gotten across the point you needed to make. If you're ever stuck on how to structure a conversation, how to write an email, or how to approach someone you need to talk to just remember: 'My name is Inigo Montoya. You killed my father. Prepare to die.'

But of course, some people understand things better through concrete examples, so let's look at how you might apply the Montoya Method through an email, letter, or social media message. We'll use the following situations as examples: someone contacting their school about accommodations, someone reaching out to a fellow advocate about collaboration, and someone writing to a legislator about voting for a bill that is currently on the floor. Keep in mind that each of these scenarios is purely hypothetical so that you can see the Montoya Method in action. Names were chosen randomly and are not intended to represent any real people.

Scenario 1: Olivia contacts her principal about school accommodations.

Dear Principal Baldwin,
My name is Olivia, and I am a student in Mrs. Carter's homeroom class. I am sending you this email because I would like to discuss my disability accommodations. As you may know, I am autistic and so I am very easily distracted by noise. It

has been helpful for me in the past to take exams outside of the classroom in a quieter place, and this accommodation has been previously approved for me. I need your help communicating this to my teachers, and it would be great if you could assist me in speaking to my teachers about this accommodation so that I am better able to take my exams.
Thank you,
Olivia

Olivia starts by introducing herself and clarifying which class (or alternatively, classes) she is a student in, providing context for what she is about to ask the principal. In just the first sentence, Olivia has already completed the first step of the Montoya Method and is beginning on the second. Olivia then completes step two by explaining what accommodations she needs and why she needs them, which frames the importance of her request. Olivia then manages expectations by directly asking the principal for help with approaching her teachers about implementing her accommodations before signing the email with a salutation and signature.

Scenario 2: John networks with another activist about collaborating.

Hi Abby,
My name is John, and I am also an advocate who is interested in fighting climate change. I saw your article about the small steps that each of us can take to reduce our carbon footprint, and I thought it was very insightful. I also run a blog that is focused on climate activism, and I was wondering if you might

be interested in writing a guest post for my blog sometime?
I think that my readers would greatly benefit from hearing
your expertise on this subject.
Thanks for your consideration,
John

Here, John begins by introducing not only himself but also the fact that he is an advocate doing similar work to Abby. John draws a personal connection by pointing out that he has read one of Abby's posts, which he was impressed with, and also clarifies that he too runs a blog. John then lays down his expectation, in this case that he would like to know if Abby would be interested in collaborating via a guest post on his blog. As usual, a salutation and signature close the email.

Scenario 3: Marco writes to a legislator about a crucial bill.

Senator Smith,
My name is Marco, and I live within the region that you were
elected to represent. It is my understanding that there is a bill
regarding local regulations on the city's power plant current-
ly on the floor that will soon be voted on. My neighborhood is
located right on the edge of the river downstream from the
power plant, and myself and many of my neighbors are very
concerned about the negative health effects that pollutants
from the plant may be having on us. I feel as though the
increased regulations stipulated in the bill will help to keep
our community safe. Therefore, I am writing to encourage
you to vote 'yes' on this bill.
Sincerely,
Marco

Marco introduces himself and then mentions that he lives within the region that Senator Smith represents, which is an important piece of political information in this context. Marco continues providing a relevant personal link by detailing why he cares about the bill on the floor and putting forward the concerns of his neighbors. Finally, Marco completes the final step of the Montoya Method in just one sentence, asking Senator Smith to vote a specific way on the bill.

When it comes down to it, reaching out to other people is anything but straightforward or easy. But because it is such an important part of being an advocate, hopefully this set of guidelines can help you get started. And of course, as with anything, it will get a little bit easier with practice.

Plagiarism

Plagiarism is the act of, either intentionally or unintentionally, passing off someone else's work or ideas as your own.[4] Unfortunately, plagiarism runs rampant on the internet, and it is a huge problem that many content creators must continuously fight. Common types of plagiarism include posting an image that somebody else created to a social media page without crediting the original creator, copying and pasting in large swathes of text written by another person without crediting the original author, restating an idea derived from

---

4   Crews, Kenneth. 'Copyright Quick Guide.' Copyright Advisory Services, Columbia University Libraries. 2015. https://copyright.columbia.edu/basics/copyright-quick-guide.html

another person without citing the original source, and closely recreating a piece of media made by another person and then posting it without reference to the original creator. Essentially, any time you publish the work of another person in a way that it could be mistaken for your own, it's plagiarism.

The first thing to know about plagiarism is that you should never ever engage in it. Don't even think about it. It's super uncool, reduces your credibility as an advocate, and can even get you into legal trouble. This doesn't mean that you can't ever use someone else's ideas; it simply means that they must be properly cited. If you want to use someone else's ideas in a piece of writing, for example, restate the idea in your own words and then reference the original source where you heard the idea and provide a way for readers to find the original source, such as by including a link or giving the name of the original source and its publisher.

What you cannot do, however, is simply copy and paste in a large block of text from another source, even if you cite where the writing originally came from. Short, direct quotes of a few sentences are generally fine so long as they are attributed as quotes, but you should largely be restating the idea in your own words rather than copying straight from the original source.

When sharing images and other similar media, you should always share directly from the original source, if possible. For example, on Twitter you should retweet someone's original tweet rather than saving the image to your device and then tweeting it out on your own. No modifications should be made to the original piece of media, including cropping. And, of course, the original creator should be separately cited. It is also good practice to ask the person in question for permission to share their work, if possible.

I have found that in most semi-casual contexts, other advocates are generally fine with their work being shared on social media in this way so long as the above guidelines are followed. However, when it comes to the topic of sharing images, videos, music, and similar sources of media you need to be extra careful because you not only have to consider plagiarism but also copyright law. Copyright essentially refers to a content creator's right to control the publication of their own work, and it means that you may not be allowed to share an image or similar media even if you properly cite and give credit to the original creator. Only specific creative works or ways of presenting ideas such as images, videos, music and audio files, scripts, and pieces of writing can be copyrighted. Ideas and concepts, although they can be plagiarized, cannot be copyrighted.

I am by no means an expert on this topic, and nothing written here should be considered any sort of legal advice. But, in a nutshell, a creative work cannot be republished by anyone except for the original creator unless the work is made available by the original creator for fair use or explicit written permission for reproduction is received from the copyright holder. A piece of media that is made available for fair use means that it can be shared and used so long as credit is given to the original creator. However, if a piece of media is not labeled for fair use then it cannot be used or shared without permission from whoever owns the copyright, typically (but not always) the original creator, even if it is properly cited and credited. And despite the common practice in the realm of YouTube Land, simply saying 'no copyright infringement intended' is not enough to subvert these rules.

It can sometimes be difficult to tell what media is available for fair use and what isn't. Some search engines offer the ability to filter an image search so that it shows only images labeled for fair use and some websites, such as Wikimedia, curate only fair-use content, but these tools may not always be completely reliable. Therefore, the safest way to prevent yourself from breaking copyright, even if accidentally, is to do one or more of the following: only use and share media that you have created as original pieces of work, only use and share media that you have explicit written permission from the copyright holder to use, or only use and share media that you have obtained a license to use (for example, purchased stock photos).

It is important to realize as well that plagiarism and even copyright infringement can happen accidentally. When I had just started my Facebook page centered around my advocacy work, I shared a few images that I had found online to my page because I liked the messaging that they contained. I did not cite the original artist simply because I did not think about it at the time. A few days later however, I was contacted by the original creator of these images, who informed me that what I had done was essentially stealing. I had unintentionally plagiarized these images from their creator. Thankfully, in this particular scenario I was able to apologize to the original creator and modify the posts so that they linked to the source of the original work and everything worked out, but on that day I learned to be much more careful about citing my sources.

By being aware of plagiarism and copyright infringement and always making sure to cite and credit your sources you may be able to prevent yourself from making a similar mistake.

Finally, if you are a content creator it is possible, and probably even likely, that your work will be plagiarized by someone else. Having your work plagiarized is essentially impossible to totally prevent if you are posting publicly online, but there are a few things you can do to help better protect yourself from it. The first is to use a watermark on visual media such as photos and videos. The watermark could be anything that identifies you, such as your name, a website, or a social media handle, and should be placed as close to the middle of the frame as possible so it cannot simply be cropped out. The downside to this method of course is that it only works well for visual media and cannot really be implemented with pieces of writing or audio such as music or podcasts.

A method that does have universal effectiveness however is to simply call out plagiarism whenever you see it. Even if it's not your own work being plagiarized, contact the person who committed the plagiarism and inform them of what has been done. It is possible that it was a mistake, or if not, it is possible that a confrontation can cause them to think twice before plagiarizing in the future. Posting publicly in the comments on the original source of the work can also be useful in calling out plagiarism. Remember also that as a content creator you own the copyright to any work that you create from the moment it is created. You don't have to register your work to gain the benefit of copyright protection. Therefore, online copyright infringements of your own work can be reported directly to the site they were posted to, as plagiarism and copyright infringement should be against the terms of service of any reputable online platform.

Logical fallacies

A logical fallacy is a formally recognized error in logic that occurs when someone is trying to use reasoning to support a specific position.[5]

It may seem like a pointless study in formal logic to take a look at logical fallacies, but understanding and being able to recognize logical fallacies will make you a better advocate. Advocating will involve defending positions that you take on certain issues, and avoiding logical fallacies is important for being able to present the strongest argument possible for your beliefs. Few things will discredit your position faster than being called out for fallacious reasoning!

On the other hand, if you find yourself having to defend your position from other people who are arguing against it, it can be helpful to look for logical fallacies in their arguments so that they can be called out to better defend your beliefs. With that in mind, let's go through a list of several different types of common logical fallacies, looking at an example of each of them and what defines them.[6]

---

5   'Logical Fallacies.' Purdue Online Writing Lab, Purdue University. https://owl.purdue.edu/owl/general_writing/academic_writing/logic_in_argumentative_writing/fallacies.html

6   Richardson, Jess, and Andy Smith, et al. 'Your Logical Fallacy Is.' The School of Thought. www.yourlogicalfallacyis.com

Straw man fallacy: This occurs when someone misrepresents another person's position, beliefs, or arguments in order to make them easier to tear down. The name alludes to going to battle against a field of straw training dummies rather than an actual army. It's super easy to win a fight against a straw man, but you're not actually fighting the real thing. This fallacy is very easy to recognize when it's used against you, but conversely it is also very easy to fall into the trap of using this fallacy yourself. To avoid committing a straw man fallacy, thoroughly research and gain a firm understanding of your opponent's position and arguments. It is advisable that you present an opponent's position with the strongest arguments possible, as this lends credibility to your own position when you are able to argue against it at full strength.

Example: 'People who prefer Pepsi over Coke only do so because they like the logo better.'

Slippery slope fallacy: This occurs when someone argues without specific evidence that taking one step will lead to a cascade of future negative steps, like sliding down a slippery slope.

Example: 'We can't allow the school to institute a new dress code. Next thing you know they'll be telling students they have to all dye their hair the same color!'

False dichotomy: This is the 'You're either with me or you're against me' fallacy. A false dichotomy occurs when only two options are presented as being valid, when in fact there are more than two possible options.

Example: 'You can either love dogs and hate cats or hate cats and love dogs, but you can't love both.'

Hasty generalization: This occurs when a generalization about a whole is made due to an attribute of one part. Stereotypes are often examples of hasty generalizations, but any time insufficient data is used to draw a conclusion about the entirety of a group it can be considered a hasty generalization.

Example: 'I was once watching a rugby game when a huge brawl erupted on the pitch. All rugby players must be very violent people!'

No true Scotsman fallacy: This occurs when someone attempts to defend their hasty generalization from a counterexample by brushing off said counterexample improperly. The name of this fallacy comes from a famous example of it that goes like this:

Person A: Scotsmen don't put sugar in their tea.

Person B: That's not true, my grandfather is a Scotsman and he puts sugar in his tea.

Person A: Then your grandfather must not be a true Scotsman, because Scotsmen don't put sugar in their tea. Another example:

Person A: Autistic people can't feel empathy.

Person B: That's not true, I'm autistic and I feel empathy very strongly.

Person A: Then you must not really be autistic, because autistic people don't feel empathy.

Moving the goalposts: This occurs when somebody shifts the burden of proof when evidence has already been provided that invalidates their position. People who move the goalposts can be frustrating to deal with because no matter what evidence is provided to them, they can continue to shift the burden of proof indefinitely.

Example:

Person A: Show me evidence that the Apollo astronauts really landed on the moon.

Person B: We can bounce lasers off of mirrors left on the moon by astronauts.

Person A: That doesn't prove anything! That data could easily be faked.

Post hoc ergo fallacy: This fallacy can be summed up as 'correlation does not equal causation.' Just because A appears to be associated with B does not mean that B is causing A.

Example: 'My child was diagnosed with autism right after getting a vaccination, so vaccines must cause autism!'

Circular reasoning: This occurs when someone attempts to defend their argument by simply restating their argument.

Example: 'The president is a good speaker because the speeches he makes are all really good.'

Bandwagon fallacy: This occurs when someone attempts to

argue that because lots of people believe a certain thing it must be true.

Example: 'The Dallas Cowboys are the best football team in America because they have the most fans.'

Ad hominem fallacy: This occurs when someone attempts to defeat an argument by attacking or insulting the person who made the argument.

Example: 'You only think that because you're stupid!'

Red herring: This occurs when someone attempts to divert attention away from an argument by bringing up something irrelevant to the argument. Basically, if a TV lawyer would shout 'Objection, relevance!' if it were used in a courtroom, then it's probably a red herring.

Example: 'Sure, my proposed budget cuts millions of dollars from education, but just look at how much money it gives to infrastructure!'

Fallacy fallacy: This occurs when someone assumes that just because a logical fallacy was used to argue for a point the point must be incorrect. Just because a point was supported with a fallacious argument does not necessarily mean the point is wrong, it could just be that it was poorly argued.

Example: 'Steven used circular reasoning to try to say that hotdogs are a type of sandwich, so obviously hotdogs must not be a type of sandwich.'

There are many other named and recognized logical fallacies

other than just these, of course, and there is much more to debate and logical argumentation than just memorizing a list of logical fallacies to avoid or look out for. But what's more important than being able to perfectly recognize fallacies is that you're thinking about the logic and reasoning behind debate.

By examining both your own arguments and those of other people through the lens of logical consistency you will start to develop critical thinking skills that will make you a better advocate. Plus, it's a lot of fun to be able to call out by name various logical fallacies when they are used against you, and learning to avoid arguing with logical fallacies will strengthen the credibility of your arguments and in turn help convince more people of your position.

The art of persistence

A common trajectory for many young advocates, especially us autistic advocates because of our brain's tendency to shift rapidly between hyperfocus and lack of interest, is to become very deeply invested in an advocacy cause for a short time before quickly losing interest, abandoning their platform, and never participating in advocacy and activism again. This is an unfortunate outcome because being an advocate is something that can be done on some scale every day for the rest of your life. This doesn't mean you have to keep up a public platform, or constantly be creating new content, or constantly be going to events. Advocacy can be thought of as a mindset; as the stubborn refusal to accept a broken status quo and the dogged desire to make change. This is a mindset that can be brought to an uncountable variety of everyday situations, not the least of which is self-advocacy, making sure that the necessary changes are made so that your needs are met.

Throughout this book we've been talking mostly about platform advocacy - having some sort of public presence through which you can promote change and take public action to make your community a better place. But you can also be an advocate by taking very simple actions, such as by spreading awareness through educating other people you come across, calling out injustices you see to those around you, voting with your conscience in elections when you are old enough, and taking small actions such as signing petitions and donating to charitable causes that you care about. As such, being an advocate is a mindset that you can carry with you long after the peak of any platform that you may develop.

The best advice that I can offer to you is this: use a deep interest in advocacy to your advantage. Go all-in while you have the passion; be active on your advocacy platform, shout out your message, write, attend events, network with other advocates, and grow your audience both within your community and beyond. If your interest in this sort of advocacy continues for the rest of your life, then that's fantastic! You might even be able to make a career out of advocating for your cause. But ultimately, even if after weeks or months or years your interest in activism starts to wane, I hope that you can continue to keep an advocacy mindset throughout the rest of your life. Don't give up on promoting what you believe in just because you become burnt out from doing platform advocacy.

Although it is true that sometimes we can be our own biggest obstacles, it's easy to become discouraged as an advocate for no fault of our own, especially when it seems like all our efforts are turning out for nothing. I'll tell you from personal experience that change, if it comes at all, comes very slowly for even the most potent advocacy movements. It can be hard to put in lots of work advocating only to see almost no results. It's also possible that people whom you are close to you, including family and close friends, will disagree with your advocacy position, and your work as an advocate may even strain your relationship with people who are close to you. Under circumstances such as these, it is no wonder that so many people lose their drive for advocacy after only a short while.

However, with the right mindset it is possible to remain persistent even in the face of slow change and personal disapproval. The first practice to put into place is to measure change in inches, not miles (or if you prefer the metric system, measure in centimeters, not kilometers). If you're looking for huge social shifts overnight then it's easy to miss positive change as it occurs on a smaller and slower level. Celebrate the smallest of victories as they come, in whatever form they may take. Something that can be helpful is to keep a notebook of the small victories you have achieved and the small changes you see every day. Whenever you feel like you've run up against a brick wall and nothing you're doing is working, simply look back through the notebook.

I encourage you to think in terms of playing the long game: being able to be a bit stubborn and keep promoting change despite the setbacks, despite the failures, and despite whatever anyone else thinks. Remember that being persistent does not involve constantly pushing yourself past your limit. Nobody completes a marathon by sprinting the entire way. Allow yourself time to rest and take breaks when you need them. Take time to take care of your mental health and listen to what your body is telling you to avoid burnout. I promise that the need for your activism will still be there when you're ready to come back.

I also encourage you to value advocacy for more than just results. Sure, the entire purpose of advocacy and activism is to create change, but the actual process of being an advocate can have many additional benefits that come with it. As you grow as an advocate, value advocacy work for what it teaches you about yourself, the experiences you get to have, and the friends you make along the way. My favorite part of being an advocate has been the fact that I have been able to connect with so many amazing people, some of whom I have become friends with. Some of my favorite memories are from when I have had the opportunity to travel to other states and other cities to give speeches and presentations. These are people that I never would have met and memories I never would have made had I not been an advocate. If you value being an advocate for these things in addition to just results, then your work will take on an entirely new personal meaning that can keep you motivated through even the toughest trials.

Concluding thoughts

Obviously, not every possible setback and obstacle that you

may encounter can be detailed here. In fact, we've barely made a dent in covering how to troubleshoot every possible problem you may encounter. But hopefully, by staying persistent and being able to continue to learn and grow, you will be able to overcome anything that stands in the way of you and your goal to help make your community a little bit of a better place. Stay persistent, be patient, and take care of yourself and there is almost nothing that you won't be able to overcome.

And with that, the guided section of this book is coming to a close. There is still much more to learn about being an advocate or an activist, but ultimately hundreds of books would need to be written to teach you everything there is to know, and I doubt that any one advocate knows all of it. However, by simply putting your best foot forward and having the courage to get out there and do your best to create change there is much that you will learn on your own as you continue your lifelong journey as an advocate.

Throughout this book, we have also had the opportunity to learn from other autistic advocates as they shared their experiences and perspectives in interviews at the end of each chapter. Hearing from other young autistic advocates has been incredibly valuable, and I hope that their insights have been helpful to you. The next and final section of this book will be composed of longer case studies featuring five additional young autistic advocates. As each of these tells their story, my hope is that you will be able to see how they implemented the strategies and techniques we have discussed in this book, gain insights into what being a young autistic advocate looks like in the real world, and be inspired by their actions.

Interview 6:
Jordyn on communication, stereotypes, and self-care

Overcoming adversity is pivotal to being a successful advocate, and no other advocates that I know of have displayed as much persistence and problem-solving prowess as our final interview subject. Jordyn is an 18-year-old nonspeaking advocate from Ontario, Canada, who communicates his thoughts through spelling. Jordyn authors the blog *Jordyn's Rocky Journey*, and has given both in-person and multi-media presentations to share his perspectives. He was also featured in an indie documentary that illustrates the disconnect between the brain and body and the importance of access to communication for autistics with similar sensory-motor challenges. Jordyn aims to increase understanding and acceptance of autistic people, especially non-, minimally, and unreliably speaking autistic people, and also hopes to fill the world with more love, peace, and joy.

Some people might be surprised to learn that a nonspeaking person can be so communicative as to run an advocacy platform. Would you care to elaborate a bit more on what it means for you to spell to communicate?

Having self-expression is a human right. I think everyone should have access to a full expressive vocabulary. Many nonspeaking autistics are bound by either being considered nonverbal (without language) or by the limits imposed on them by a picture-based communication system. Communication that is alphabet-based gives me the freedom to express my ideas, thoughts, opinions, wants, and feelings fully, consistent with how I formulate them in my head. Imagine having a choice-based life or no choice at all - by limiting expression the world of my fellow nonspeakers is limited.

My wise words would never have been 'heard' had I not been taught to slow my impulsive body down so what I pointed to was what I intended. Spelling unlocked a whole world and allows me to contribute to society in a meaningful way!

Stereotypes can be very frustrating to deal with as an autistic advocate. What are some of the most frequent untrue stereotypes that you find yourself having to face as an advocate, and how have you gone about dispelling or overcoming them in the past? Additionally, in the past, have you ever found yourself in a situation where it was difficult to get people to listen to your voice or take you seriously? If so, what strategies did you use to help make yourself heard?

I think I have been lucky to not have been subjected to too many environments where untrue stereotypes are ingrained in the culture. Normal, caring people who have been misinformed are the people I encounter. Those well-intentioned folks who either talk about me with me right there or change their affect when addressing me to some slow, articulate, simple-worded version of what they intend to convey. Mostly, my Communication Partner ignores anything addressed to them instead of me and has me answer. This handles the situation effectively most of the time. These folks self-correct when they see the dynamic unfold in front of them and how I express myself.

On the occasions where they don't self-correct, I correct them. Sometimes people are not self-aware or are obliviously on automatic and need a little jolt awake. I find humor is also a very effective tool in all of these instances.

Additionally, where this kind of thing could garner anger or upset from me, I live to be a demonstration in presuming competence. So, I believe being compassionate and understanding of their actions resulting from being misinformed is paramount. If someone is blatantly called out as wrong, defence and/or embarrassment kick in, and change is far less likely in a fight or flight state.

And sometimes, none of the above makes a difference immediately and I let it go! I must just trust that a seed has been planted and remove myself from the situation gracefully.

What self-care strategies do you use to manage your mental health, emotions, and energy while doing advocacy work?

I have learned the hard way to be very judicious with my time and energy. When I was first able to express all that had been welling up in me over my years of silence, I wanted to make a huge impact for my community. I chose to write a weekly blog as one way to consistently be an advocate for other people's access to communication and an empowering environment. I also looked for, and created, opportunities in my immediate area to expand community.

Going full out with these endeavors - ensuring questions

were answered, comments acknowledged, and every peer felt gotten and appreciated at in-person gatherings - was a full-time, exhausting undertaking. I pushed myself beyond my limits. While this was possible short-term, long-term it was going to be detrimental to the difference that I wanted to make. I needed to find balance.

I stopped posting weekly and started to post only when I had something I needed to say. I stopped trying to be present throughout long conference days and chose only the talks that I wanted to be present for, leaving to recharge in my hotel room in between. I stopped feeling like I had to be the connector of community locally and ensured my being at events was nourishing for me too. Caring for my reservoir of energy, so I could effectively utilize it, became a priority.

I have had to let go and let others pick up the baton in areas of advocacy that are more their passion than mine. I have had to clearly communicate when I can't be in proximity to others, including ensuring my mom's clients know that I have veto power on their time with her. Being me in this energetically and emotionally sensitive body means being careful who is in my space.

On a concrete front, I have learned to build a lot of recharge time into life. I have learned to slow down my beautifully committed and passionate mom and Communication Regulation Partner. I don't engage in draining, negatively charged drama, and manage those around me to be clear about their beliefs and perspectives that spin what is happening into drama or creates negative context. Lots of flipping automatic ingrained negative filters for those close to me is my gift to them and me. Challenges become opportunities around me, and I hope that demonstration causes a ripple effect.

What advice, if any, would you give to an aspiring young autistic advocate who wants to make change in the world?

- **Share from your heart and your experience.** I believe being relatable is paramount to engaging an audience. Listening to you should be a pleasure and take them on a journey where they can draw parallels to their own lives. No one wants to be talked at or preached to. Let people in and let them create their own learning.
- **Get clear about your message and your specific mission.** While this may change and evolve, your general theme and message need to be clear as people want to know the intention of who they are listening to. Being a brand of advocate they can trust to deliver will have them come back for your take on aspects of your intended overall theme.
- **Create a team around you that empowers you.** I love that when I have a crazy idea my badass peeps go with it. They trust that my loving steps to achieve something are thought through and may get caringly to the destination on a route they hadn't considered. They also allow me to make mistakes and learn from them. Just getting me to have my creations come alive by being my partners is their goal. Additionally, they have learned not to push or force my process, letting me create or recharge at my own pace.

- **Balance and fun are a must!** I think we tend to sometimes want to take on the world and eradicate injustice with gusto. Being passionate and driven is great; however, it isn't everything. I learned the hard way that burnout is real, and living to advocate got so hard. If it isn't nourishing, my advice is drop it, scale back, and wait to be inspired while filling life with activities that fill your tank.

Jordyn can be found online at the following:

Facebook: Jordyn's 'Rocky' Journey[7]

On the web: www.jordynsrockyjourney.wordpress.com

---

[7] www.facebook.com/jordynsrockyjourney

Advocacy Case Studies

If there is one thing that I hope you have figured out by now, it is that advocacy and activism can take on a range of forms depending on your topic, your audience, your methods, and a variety of other factors determined by your unique situation. No two advocates' journeys will be alike, and what has worked in the past for one person may not be applicable to everyone else. Throughout this book, the information and advice I have given you is based primarily on my own experience as an autism and neurodiversity advocate, as well as observations about what I have seen work for others. And, of course, we have also had the opportunity to gain insight directly from six young autistic advocates through the interviews placed at the end of each chapter.

However, before we depart I would like to give you a better idea of what being an advocate looks like, as told by other real-world activists. This last chapter will be dedicated to case studies with five young autistic advocates. As you read their stories, I hope that you can start to get a sense of what being an advocate as an autistic young person is like: the obstacles you may face, the sorts of challenges and triumphs you might expect, the process of creating and managing an advocacy platform, and what you can do to move past obstacles and continue creating change in your community.

I hope that the stories of these advocates, and those interviewed earlier, will inspire you to take action for the issues that you care about, if you haven't already. I hope they can provide you with additional guidance and insight as you embark on your own journey. I hope that these stories will make you feel empowered and emboldened to be the one who makes the change that you desire to see, and that you will come away confident in the knowledge that everyone, including yourself, can be an advocate, in whatever unique way that looks like for you.

In each of the following case studies, the questions presented in my own words will be in *italics* while the words of the case study's subject will be in normal text.

Siena Castellon

Background:

Our first case study features 19-year-old multi-award-winning neurodiversity advocate Siena Castellon from London in the United Kingdom. Siena is perhaps most notable for founding Neurodiversity Celebration Week, an annual global event involving thousands of schools and hundreds of thousands of students that aims to showcase the positive aspects of neurodiversity and empower neurodiverse students. In addition to being a public speaker and social media influencer, Siena is also the author of *The Spectrum Girl's Survival Guide,* the first book aimed at autistic girls, written by an autistic girl. Siena has been diagnosed with autism, ADHD, dyslexia, and dyspraxia.

So let's go all the way back to the beginning. What made you start to think that you wanted to be an advocate? That you wanted to inspire change? Was there a series of events that led up to that?

I've had an interesting journey from a neurodiversity perspective. I'm autistic, dyslexic, dyspraxic, and I have ADHD. For most of my school experience I was undiagnosed and spent a lot of time wondering why I was different. I was aware that I was the only person who was struggling with social interaction and engagement. For example, I had minimal facial expressions, didn't have intonation in my voice, and I struggled to make sense of body language. Although these skills seemed to come effortlessly to everyone else, they were a mystery to me.

Since I knew I was different to everyone else, I grew up trying to decipher why I was different and trying to find an answer as to what was wrong with me.

Growing up feeling disconnected and different from everyone else is a very isolating experience. At the time, I believed I was the only person going through this. It wasn't until I was diagnosed as being autistic when I was 12 that a whole new world opened up for me. I discovered that I really wasn't that alone after all and that the alienation I had felt growing up was a very common experience for autistic individuals.

To this day, I never cease to be shocked at the similarities in your stories and experiences. For example, I attended

11 schools because I was either relentlessly bullied or my teachers did not have any experience in supporting students with neurological differences. I was even home educated for a few months because I was suffering from school-related PTSD. It wasn't until I met other autistic individuals that I realized that my story wasn't unique. In fact, it was pretty common because mainstream education isn't designed to cater for or support neurodivergent students.

It was around this time that I realized that there weren't any resources aimed at supporting neurodivergent students. The few organizations that were supporting neurodiversity were aimed at parents of children with learning differences. None of the websites were focused on empowering and supporting children and young people. I also found that the organizations focused on the negatives and perceived deficits of having a neurodivergent child, which was creating a negative and imbalanced narrative about neurodiversity.

I realized that I had the potential to make a significant difference in the way neurodivergent youth felt about themselves if I dedicated myself to creating a more balanced and positive image of neurodiversity that identified challenges but also celebrated talents and strengths. I also felt that as a young, neurodivergent student who was navigating the educational system, my voice and experiences would be more relatable and engaging than if the tips and advice were coming from a neurotypical middle-aged man with a psychology degree. So when I was 13, I created my first website - QLMentoring. When I started it, I hoped that sharing the tips and tricks I used to help me to succeed in school would benefit neurodivergent children who may have been feeling isolated and alone in their struggles.

So would you say that you saw an empty niche, and then filled it?

Definitely. Although 20 percent of the population is neuro-divergent, very few businesses and organizations cater to our needs. It still shocks me that most classroom teachers receive little or no training on how to identify or support their neurodivergent students. This approach is hard to justify when you consider that one in five students in every classroom has a neurological difference. Instead of adapting our education system so that it can be inclusive of different learning styles, the system is designed in such a way as to ensure that many neurodivergent students underperform and fail to achieve their academic potential. It's almost as if our education system views us as expendable.

What made you decide on a website over some sort of other campaign? Was it the accessibility? Or just what you knew? Did it just seem the easiest? How did you initially go about the thought process of launching your first site?

For starters, I didn't have any role models or exposure to people who were advocates. I'm also a naturally shy and reserved person and so I would never have seen myself taking on that type of role. I was basically on my own and figuring things out as best as I could. The appeal of creating a website was that it didn't involve social interaction. It gave me the freedom to create the type of information and resources that I wish had been available and that I would have found helpful. It also allowed me to stay within my comfort zone, while still making a difference. My advocacy gradually grew from there and so did my confidence and belief in myself. Looking back, I don't think I would have been ready at the age of 13 to fully put myself out there in the public eye, at least not in the same way that I am now able to. One lesson I learnt is that advocates aren't born, they are made. If you're really passionate about something, you'll find a way to make your voice heard.

So you have your website up. I imagine that, like anybody, when you first started you had a relatively small reach. So how did you go from having created this resource, to getting it out into the world in the very beginning? Did you share it with friends? Did you post about it on social media? What did that look like?

Since I had very limited resources, I realized that I would have to market my website and budding advocacy on social media. I began by following autistic charities and similar organizations, as well as prominent neurodiversity advocates. I started by posting my website content and also reposting ND information I found engaging and informative. Over several years, I gradually built up a following of like-minded people on Twitter and later on LinkedIn and Instagram. I also reached out to ND organizations and ND magazines offering to write articles, such as back-to-school articles. Furthermore, I focused on looking for other complementary opportunities that could amplify my advocacy, such as applying to be on the National Anti-Bullying Youth Board. Serving on the Youth

Board opened up a lot of opportunities and taught me valuable skills. As I began making a name for myself, I discovered that youth organizations were keen to work with me because neurodiversity rights, equality, and acceptance was an overlooked area that they hadn't previously focused on. In many ways, I was filling a gap in the market that they didn't know had existed.

I think it's important to emphasize that my advocacy didn't happen overnight. It took years of networking and establishing connections with like-minded people to culminate in where I find myself today. So, when people ask me 'How do I become an advocate?' I tell them to find something that are really passionate about and take it one step at a time. The first step is always the hardest because you are venturing into the unknown, but after that each step becomes easier.

Did you feel like in the beginning, there was a moment when you started seeing a larger volume of emails? Like an exponential growth of your platform sort of thing? Or did it happen more slowly?

It was much more gradual than that. I had a few spikes here and there. For example, after I won the BBC Teen Hero Award and was featured on national television I saw a spike in emails and website subscribers.

When I was 16, I launched Neurodiversity Celebration Week. This also coincided with signing a book deal. The first year I ran Neurodiversity Celebration Week, I had 100 schools take part. At the time, I was over the moon. Two years later, I had over 1500 schools take part. I believe that being selected by the United Nations to be a Young Leader for the SDGs [Sustainable Development Goals], as well as the success of my book, helped to give me the credibility and prominence I needed to take Neurodiversity Celebration Week to the next level.

What was the first award that you won, and how did you get yourself nominated for it?

The first award I won was the 2017 BDA Young Person's Award from the British Dyslexia Association. I believe my mum nominated me. It was a huge moment for me because it was the first time I was around people who viewed dyslexia as a strength and a positive.

Later on, I would be nominated for awards by people I had helped or whom I had worked with. For example, when I was 16, I received an email from a lady who had two autistic grandchildren and had found my website very informative and helpful. She asked me if she could nominate me to take part in the Lions Club Young Ambassador competition. The competition involved presenting my neurodiversity project, giving a speech, and being interviewed by a panel of judges. I agreed to take part and ended up winning the local and national competition. I ended up representing the British Isles in the Lions Club European Finals in Tallin, Estonia, which was surreal. It was an amazing experience that I will always look back on with fondness.

I imagine for a lot of these awards, especially the ones you won early on in your career, you did nominate yourself, and I imagine

*that for speaking opportunities it was similar in that it was you
who reached out and asked to speak?*

I think that some of it was just a snowball kind of effect.
I was invited to give one talk and there were people in the
audience who heard me and then referred me to give another
talk. I mean, a lot of the time I would give a speech and then
get contacted by other people immediately after and they'd
say, 'Hey, we'd love to have you give a talk to our organization.'
I was also offering my services for free so I think that also
helped. But I think the reason people connected with me was
that I was providing a different narrative and perspective. I
was a teenager with lived experience talking about what it's
like to be a student in our education system. I was much more
relatable and real because I was talking about something I
was living and experiencing. This was a stark contrast from
listening to trained psychologists or clinical neurotypical
adults talking about a subject they've only studied and learnt
about in books.

*The question I'm trying to get at I guess is, very early on, how did
you make this transition from just a kid with a website to someone who is being sought out and asked to come give talks?*

It's been six years since I launched my first website. There
isn't one particular moment that I can pinpoint as the tipping
point. It really was a slow burn and a gradual build up. As
I mentioned earlier, the publication of my book definitely
helped because it opened me up to a whole new audience. My
role as a Young Leader for the SDGs also helped to give me

further prominence by giving me global opportunities I never could have imagined. For example, the UN invited me to give a talk during their Global Autism Awareness Day event.

As my prominence in the neurodiversity sector grew so did Neurodiversity Celebration Week. Last year over 1500 schools and 200 businesses and organizations took part. The UK Royal Navy even recorded a video, which was surreal!

One thing I've learnt is to never underestimate how small the world is. Once you build your network and establish a reputation for yourself you begin to realize that the community isn't as big as you once thought. If there is one bit of advice I wish I had had early on, it is to identify key players and like-minded people to reach out to. I've found that most people are very helpful and keen to encourage and support the next generation of advocates and youth leaders.

You've previously mentioned that when you were 14 and you were giving presentations and speeches, you would have panic attacks, and I know that you've told me before that in the past you had a lot of trouble with public speaking. How did you overcome that? Did it take a lot of practice, or do you have specific strategies that you use?

I'm a naturally shy and soft-spoken person. At school, I would blend into the background. If someone had told me that I would one day be giving speeches at the UN and giving presentations to organizations like AstraZeneca and the UK Ministry of Defence, I wouldn't have believed them. I think the fact that it happened gradually helped. The more presentations I did, the less anxious I became. Eventually, I learned not to be too hard on myself and no to expect perfection. I recognize that I am not the best public speaker, but that doesn't mean that I don't have important things to say and that I shouldn't use my voice to bring about change.

I remember one moment that was a turning point for my public speaking. It was the BBC Teen Hero Awards - a live event that was aired to millions of households across the UK. I had to go on stage in front of an audience of 10,000 people to accept the award and give a short speech. I had memorized and rehearsed my short speech. However, when the time came for me to get on stage, I was asked to crawl into a trap door beneath the stage that was filled with dry ice and told that the contraption would elevate me onto the stage. As I was slowly elevated onto the stage, I was surrounded by smoke, blasted with music and bright lights and the thunder of thousands of voices cheering. As an autistic person who is sensitive to lights and sounds it was my worst nightmare! I was so focused on trying to maintain my composure (when I was in deep sensory distress) that I completely forgot my speech. When I was handed the microphone and it was time to give my speech, I had no choice but to make it up on the spot. I gave a short speech about the importance of being kind and accepting people for who they are. It got a massive applause. My speech really resonated with the audience. To this day, it is one of the speeches I'm proudest of, because every fiber of my being was telling me to run off the stage and yet I stood my ground and made my voice heard. A few weeks later, I was contacted by a production team who wanted me to feature in a Carmen Sandiego series featuring advocates from around the world. They told me that they had watched the Teen Hero Awards and had been really impressed by my speech.

I've seen the video, and I will admit that you are very obviously, like, deer in the headlights.

I watch it now with equal measure of horror and pride. I remember how stressed and distressed I was at the time, but also how elated and invincible I felt after having persevered and risen to the challenge. It gave me a confidence and belief in myself that I never thought I would have.

To promote your voice and your vision as an advocate, the mediums that you have used have been primarily things like public speaking and social media outreach. How did you settle on using these to get your ideas out into the world?

Yeah, I think that the big realization I had was that I needed to find people who wanted to hear my message. I needed to find my target audience, the people who would benefit from hearing my message and story. So, I had to seek out those communities and build relationships with like-minded people. I began by reaching out to people on Twitter and other social platforms. I focused on establishing contacts and relationships with established organizations, such as the British Dyslexia Association and the ADHD Foundation. Whenever I read an interesting article, I would research the author and reach out to them via social media or email. I wasn't afraid to reach out to people and in the process discovered that most people were really helpful and supportive of my advocacy.

Given how young I was, I didn't begin meeting people in person until I was older and, even then, I was always accompanied by my mum. Now that Zoom has become mainstream, this is another platform that the next generations can use to promote their advocacy.

So it was the community that drew you in?

As someone who grew up feeling isolated and alone, it was transformative to find a community that understood me and that I could relate to. The commonalities that we share, in terms of being rejected, bullied, misunderstood, etc., are experiences that bond us. I was 15 when I first met another autistic girl. I had been led to believe we were a rarity. But it turns out there is a whole community of autistic women and that there are many more of us out there that are yet to be diagnosed. The knowledge that there were others out there like me was the first time I felt a sense of belonging.

Would you like to talk a little bit more about how Neurodiversity Celebration Week came about?

Early on in my advocacy, I realized that I wanted to change the narrative around neurodiversity. My experience had been that schools focused on negative aspects of having a learning difference. There were also lots of stereotypes and misconceptions about learning differences. The fact that most classroom teachers didn't receive any training on neurodiversity meant that many relied on these outdated stereotypes and prejudices. I had teachers who lowered their expectations as soon as they learnt I was dyslexic. It was as if they equated being dyslexic with being less intelligent, which is not the case. I also found that we were often made to feel ashamed of our neurological difference and we were often bullied for our differences. For example, students freely used the word 'autistic' as an insult and slur. I felt that the neurodivergent community wasn't being given the respect and protection that other minority groups had, such as, for example, the LGBTQ.

I launched Neurodiversity Celebration Week to change the way schools view and treat their neurodivergent students. I wanted to change the conversation so that instead of just focusing on what we struggle with and are bad at, schools also recognized and acknowledged our many strengths and talents. In order for schools to be truly inclusive, they need to support, encourage, and empower *all* their students to reach their potential. I felt that schools were failing neurodivergent students and that it was finally time to address this.

In addition to wanting to help schools to adopt a more balanced and constructive view of neurodiversity, I also wanted to provide resources to teachers who currently do not have to tools to better understand and support their students. Another aim I had was that I wanted to empower neurodivergent students to stop seeing their neurological difference as a hindrance and something to be ashamed of. Instead, I wanted to help them recognize and celebrate the many strengths and advantages that come from seeing the world differently. The reality is that neurodivergent people have revolutionized the world we live in. Some of the most successful and innovative companies, such as Apple, Tesla, Ikea, Microsoft, Dyson, HP, and Walt Disney, were founded by neurodivergent individuals. Yet, this wasn't ever mentioned or talked about. I think it's really important to give young people hope and to believe in them. Yet, sadly, my experience in school is that we were often written off. So, I decided I wanted to do something about it in the hope that I could make a positive difference to future generations of neurodivergent students.

One thing that a lot of neurodiverse people have to deal with is stereotyping. As an advocate, have you ever had to deal with people having harmful stereotypes of you and how did you overcome those?

I've had to deal with negative stereotypes and misconceptions my whole life. Back before we were using Zoom, back when most meetings were in person, people would come up to me to try to compliment me. I know they meant well, but they would say things like 'You must be really high functioning' or 'You must have a mild version of autism.' Someone actually told me that if I wanted to I could pass off as 'normal.' Someone else once told me that I should teach other autistic people to be more like me. I've had people ask me whether I am really autistic for several reasons, including that I can make eye contact, can communicate, and am a girl. There are still people out there who think that girls can't be autistic.

I used to take offense at some of the comments. But now I try to read the room and the situation. If I feel like I can educate the person, I will try to do so in a friendly and non-confrontational way. Other times I make a note to incorporate some of the examples in later speeches or events I do so that I can begin to chip away at the misconceptions and stereotypes that are still so deeply embedded into the fabric of our society.

A lot of your advocacy activities, in fact I think most of them, have centered around being online and connecting with people through social media, and using the internet, and going to these different events full of strangers you don't know, and answering emails from strangers you don't know. The unfortunate truth is that for a young person especially this can be pretty dangerous. There are a lot of bad people out there that are looking to take advantage of young people, and disabled people, and just generally being on the internet can be sort of dangerous. How did you keep yourself safe? What did you rely on to ensure that you were safe on social media and safe at the events you attended?

It was more of a concern when I was in my early teens. I remember I had started QLMentoring when I was at one school and about five months after I started it I moved to another school. At my new school, I told my director of studies about my QLMentoring site and she said she would check out my website. At our next meeting, she told me that I needed to be really careful and that I shouldn't use my name online.

One thing that I will always credit my mum for is that until recently I haven't gone to any in-person event that she didn't accompany me to. She would have to approve every event beforehand and would attend all of them with me. She would drive me most of the time, because right before I gave a speech I would get really nervous and couldn't cope with the sensory distress of using public transport.

On Twitter I have had a bit of abuse from people, but it hasn't been that bad. I've been lucky in that I have a great support network on Twitter who have always come to my defense. I have also made a conscious effort to take a professional approach to my social media, so I rarely share any private information and I rarely post selfies or other personal information. I've also learnt to liberally use the block button. Sadly, sometimes it's just better to concede that you can't change everyone's mind and that some people just aren't very nice.

As one might say, people with a chip on their shoulder?

Unfortunately, Twitter and other forms of social media can bring out the worst in some people. There are people that say some very hateful things. In the past, I invested time in trying to change their minds. But I soon realized that these types of people enjoy causing discord and division. Sadly, nothing you say or do will change their minds. So, I've learned to cut my losses and focus my time and energy on people who are open and receptive to learning about neurodiversity.

What do you see foresee as being the future of your advocacy platform?

I see Neurodiversity Celebration Week becoming bigger and better and making an even bigger impact. I am currently exploring various opportunities, including partnerships with established organizations that have the expertise and resources to take it to the next level. Up until now it's been a one-person operation that I have self-funded. So, imagine what Neurodiversity Celebration Week could become if I joined forces with an organization that will devote a team to helping run and manage the campaign.

During lockdown, I wrote a companion book to my first book, *The Spectrum Girls Survival Guide: How to Grow Up Awesome and Autistic*. My new book, *The Spectrum Girl's Survival Toolkit: The Workbook for Autistic Girls*, was recently published. I may decide to write another book, but for now I'm taking some time away from my advocacy to focus on being a university student and enjoying my last year of being a teenager.

Siena can be found online at the following:
Twitter: @qlmentoring, @NCWeek
Instagram: @qlmentoring
On the web: www.qlmentoring.com, www.sienacastellon.com

Charlie Baker

Background:
This next case study features Charlie Baker, a 20-year-old autism advocate from Maesteg, Wales, in the United Kingdom. Charlie has helped to reduce stigma about autism and neurodiversity by volunteering to mentor young people for the nonprofit Special Families and helped host a radio station at a local hospital by sharing his story and ideas in a podcast

format. Charlie's activism has led to him being given an award for community service by the mayor of his town.

You mentioned earlier to me that very early on you were struggling at school and with depression. What do you think was causing you to be in this low place?

I definitely think it had to do with the social surroundings and the environment I was in, which wasn't quite aware of my difficulties. Also, back then it was more unnoticed than it is now. When I would have these sort of meltdowns or cases of just oversensitivity within my surroundings, nobody really knew what to do and I was just sort of told off for it, for reacting in a way that I felt like I couldn't react. Because I was still young and I didn't know what was the issue, I found it difficult to really explain that to other people.

I totally relate to the reaction piece of that, and also just a lack of other people getting at what is going on. Were you undiagnosed at that time?

I was undiagnosed up until the age of I think 15 because it was a long process to actually get diagnosed. I went through CAMHS [Child and Adolescent Mental Health Services] and I had to go to my local hospital to talk to their staff as well, and that took a period of I think about four years, so I think the diagnosing process started when I was 11 and actually got finished and properly finalized when I was 15 because it was noticed right at the end of primary school, so in Year 6 when I was about 11.

Did you think that getting a diagnosis was helpful for you? Did it improve your quality of life?

Definitely! It gave me answers to a lot of questions that I had grown up wondering, like why I was so different to the kids around me, and why I was sort of unable to find that place where I could fit in. I felt extremely outcasted, and not knowing the reason behind it or the reason for my actions only sort of made it worse, so getting that diagnosis was a relief.

At some point you got interested in advocacy, and as you described, reducing the stigma around autism. Did you feel like after you were diagnosed, even though you had a quality-of-life improvement, there was more stigma that you were facing?

Personally, I didn't have any sort of negativity going through my head of 'Oh, I'm diagnosed with this now' because simply being told the answer to why I was behaving in that way was anything but negative. I've experienced weird comments, like when I tell people I'm autistic they say, 'You don't look autistic,' and I feel that's such a stupid thing to say. There are so many different variations of autism, and it doesn't seem like people want to really understand that. It is infuriating at times to sort of get that sort of response out of people.

So it was that sort of misunderstanding that you were encountering that really drove you to want to, would you say, change people's minds? Or raise more awareness? How would you describe your thought process of what you wanted to try to accomplish?

So, while I was in senior school I went through a process of getting an autism specialist on campus who already worked at the school; however, to say they did a good job is a massive overstatement because there were a lot of things I didn't like and whenever I'd try to talk to them about it, it always turned into a debate or argument, and it would mostly lead me to having meltdowns in the place where I was supposed to feel safe. It was that sort of experience that was enough for me to be like, 'I don't want other people to go through that.' Even if it's just one person I'm able to sort of give a better perspective on themselves and autism and a better understanding of how to cope with it; that's good enough for me.

Did you have one sort of moment where you decided that you wanted to be an advocate, or do you feel like you sort of fell into that role involuntarily?

I'd definitely say there were a lot of points where I felt like I could do a better job because I am someone with autism. Having someone tell me how to deal with my autism when they don't have it or have any understanding other than a textbook one of what autism is did make me want to go out there and try to do something, and that alone gave me motivation to do voluntary work, and it was then that I found the opportunity to work with Special Families, the youth club with young people.

Regarding these volunteer opportunities with the youth club, did you have to go out of your way to search for them, or did they sort of find you?

Well, I went to a place, basically the hub for any sort of charities or companies that are looking for volunteers to do such work, and I told them a little bit about myself and then they presented me with some work that was available. I think there was also some dog walking that was available and working with the RSPCA, but I ended up not going with that bit and instead reached out to the stuff around autism because that felt a lot closer to home.

Were you looking specifically to change things in your local community or town?

Oh yeah!

So your volunteer work led you to getting an award from the mayor of your town?

See, it's really difficult to think about that sort of time because I don't really remember much of it. It was rewarding, but it was also something that, yes although it is an award and I should be proud, I don't really like acknowledging it too much because to me that's sort of like, 'Oh, I've done it all now,' but that's not the case at all. There's still so much I want to do and so many more ways I could be doing better to turn away the stigma of autism.

In order to gain the recognition to get such an award or to have the opportunities for making change that you have had, you have to have some way of promoting your ideas and your platform. How have you spread your ideas out into your community?

There was also another volunteer role I was doing at the same time for a hospital radio around the area. There was a show me and a couple of other people did called *Teen Voice* where they were going for the Duke of Edinburgh Award, which includes doing a bunch of different charitable works, but my side of it was that I'm interested in media as well as the creative industry, so I sort of found a way to merge both my interest in improving the outlook for autism and my creative industry goals together.

Very nice! I'm not super familiar with how your radio program worked, but did you give little titbits, or was it more of a podcast format?

More of a podcast format for sure. It was played within the hospital at a certain time, and also there was an app you could download in the UK to listen in wherever and whenever.

So you took the volunteer opportunities you had and combined them with your interest in entertainment and media to get your voice out there?

Yeah!

Do you think that you would have had that opportunity had you not had an interest in media, or do you think you would have found that platform anyway?

See, that's an interesting thought that I have still because I would also play my last year in senior school as a reason for why I have done the things I have since, because in my last year of senior school I dropped out during the first term and only came in for the exams, so I left school with no qualifications whatsoever. I also knew that if I wanted to get somewhere I would have to properly put myself out there and show that, hey, look, although I didn't get the qualifications I wanted in school I'm still able to go out there and do these voluntary works while also doing my college courses.

Did you run into any issues with the radio station, like maybe haters or nay-sayers who discredited what you were saying?

It went smoothly generally. There wasn't much communication between me on the show with the people actually running it because at the end of the day it's a hospital, so they're mostly concerned with stuff going on in there and not necessarily the entertainment.

But, see, no matter what walk of life you go to there will always be people with different opinions. My sort of attitude has been built up over the years of growth and the experiences I've gone through. It's to just notice when there is an online troll, or there are people who are being too judgmental, that they are too closed minded to even hear me out, so I do try to avoid those types of people and give my attention to people who actually do want to know more.

You talked earlier about there being a lot more that you want to do. What do you see as being the future for your advocacy?

I would love to eventually be like a Twitch streamer, where

although the actual sort of entertainment side of it won't be around autism I'll use that to sort of build up a base of followers and then promote the better messages and be able to share my story, because if the people are following me then they're aware of my story; they're aware of my autism and my difficulties with people in general who have a worse outlook on autism.

Is there anything you feel like we've missed that you'd like to talk about?

I guess I want to say that there were extreme lows in my life. Even now there are. There are certain ways that I am able to cope with certain feelings and emotions, but other times I do rely on outside help such as medication or reaching out to charities that work in that sort of area. I think the fact that I left school with no qualifications and have basically been told that I'm a slacker and I'm not going to get anywhere (and I forget this so I have to be constantly reminded by my mother), but now I'm going to university in an area that I am very well equipped in, which is advertising design, and I have plenty of design work and knowledge on that matter – I do feel like my future is secure and I feel a lot safer because of it. I'll be going independent in September [*of 2021*] and living on my own.

I think it's important to remember that everyone's different and you don't have to force yourself to conform to someone else's timeline or standards. I bet that advertising degree will come in handy later if you want to continue to promote your message.

For sure, and being able to understand the algorithms as well on social media would be another factor into getting that sort of message out there.

Speaking of which, what do you think is the key with social media to promoting an idea or particular bit of advocacy when you're competing against all the millions of other people who are also shouting at the top of their lungs into the internet? Do you have any tips in this area?

Well, I haven't gone viral with anything so I don't have any sort of knowledge on having a proper big impact on the social platforms, but I would definitely assume that working your way around different communities and getting yourself involved with them and understanding what they're fighting for, and also telling them about yourself is a good sort of way to promote it.

Finally, are there any pieces of specific advice you'd like to give to a young autistic aspiring advocate? What would you say to them if they were standing in front of you right now?

Don't put that much pressure on yourself with thinking that you're going to change the world. Always start with what you are capable of doing and that's the community around you. Starting with what's around you is the most important part, because if you go out with the outlook of 'Oh I'm going to change the world' you're setting yourself up for a big fall in all honesty. It could be the reason why you either stop or feel like giving up. Always start with a smaller goal that is reachable, because you're more likely to get to that and then you can go up from there. It's about building the foundation and then slowly stacking blocks up instead of just immediately trying to go for the top of it.

Charlie can be found online at the following:
Instagram: @Charlie_needs_a_job

Alfie Bowen

Background:
The subject of our next case study is Alfie Bowen, an 18-year-old award-winning wildlife photographer and autism advocate from Beccles, England. Alfie uses his prowess in the art of photography as a medium for both self-expression and advocacy, framing through his lenses the wild animals that inspired him to work through his lowest times and using these stunning photographs to promote wildlife conservation, all while reminding the world of the talents and capabilities of autistic people. Alfie has worked closely with the World Wildlife Fund and other wildlife and biodiversity conservation organizations. In his debut book *Wild World: Nature through an Autistic Eye*,[1] Alfie chronicles his journey as an autistic person and environmental campaigner while showcasing some of his best photographs.

---

[1] Bowen, Alfie. *Wild World: Nature through an Autistic Eye*. Woodbridge: ACC Art Books. 2021.

Your most powerful advocacy tool has clearly been your camera. How did you first become interested in photography?

It really started out as a way to explore my obsession with animals. I came across Mum's little compact Lumix camera and picked that up, and that's where it all started when I was 15.

Did your interest in in wildlife conservation also come early on, or did that come later as an extension of being close to animals?

That's something that grew down the line really. At a younger age I suppose I wasn't really aware of that side of things. I just liked going to the zoo to look at animals and learn about animals. My first word was actually 'mallard' after the duck, when I was really young.

Was there a particular moment you can remember where you decided that you were going to be an activist, or did it sort of grow out of your photography hobby naturally?

A bit of both, I guess. I was aware when I was young that there weren't really many other autistic people that I knew of who I could look up to. The main one for me was Chris Packham, the autistic TV presenter who presents *Springwatch* over here. So I kind of realized that I would like there to be more autistic role models, and once my photography kind of took off I realized that I now had this opportunity to speak out and raise awareness.

What do you think was the impact of having someone like Chris Packham to look up to, or alternatively what do you think would have been the impact of picking a strong autistic role model?

Well, feeling less alien I guess. I always felt like I was an alien, especially in mainstream school. Looking up to people who are like you makes you feel like you're not alone.

I totally agree! Do you think that any aspect of you being autistic contributed towards your interest in photography or animals, or sort of pushed you towards your work in conservation activism?

I think that the autism is probably why I have such a strong obsession with animals. I suppose that obsession could be with anything. I guess the autism helps with the photography because I notice every tiny little detail and I notice things that others probably wouldn't, so then I photograph things in ways that other people wouldn't.

So, in a sense, being autistic makes you a better photographer?

Yeah, that's what I find anyway.

Has your artform in that sense then helped to boost your self-confidence, because it's something that you know that you're good at?

Yeah, and a lot of people are interested in it as well. That gets me talking to other people, which has really helped my social skills over the last three or four years.

So you're doing photography and taking pictures of animals and getting better at your craft. At some point down the road you become notable for using photography to advance your advocacy message. What do you think was your first advocacy project? When did it go from just pictures of animals to pictures of animals that make a difference?

I suppose it was when I got contacted by the local newspaper really, and they interviewed me. And then I thought I should be honest and open about who I am, my autism and so on. Then it kind of snowballed from there really.

The newspaper contacted you, so they must have known about your work in some capacity?

Yeah, I was on Instagram quite early on. I had quite a small audience then, but obviously the local newspaper in my little town picked up on it.

Let's talk a little bit about your medium. Photography that makes a difference. Some people may have a little bit of trouble getting the connection of how you can just have pictures but have them influence change. Can you talk a little bit about the power behind the visual art forms and how they can be as effective as, say, writing a blog maybe? They say a picture's worth a thousand words. What does that mean to you?

Well, firstly, I work quite differently to a lot of photographers whereby my autistic brain never stops, so I'll have image ideas come into my mind at two in the morning and I'll sketch them out. Then I'll go out to the field and spend however many hours until I turn that photograph from a drawing into an actual photograph, rather than like most photographers going out there and reacting to what's in front of them. I have a preconceived idea. So I guess the autism is threaded through the photographs in that sense.

I guess photography is a language that everyone can understand in all corners of the world. And then people see those images and they want to learn more about who took them, so then they start learning more about me and my autism, which in turns educates them about autism.

So you get like multiple advocacy angles. You get wildlife conservation and autism advocacy in one medium?

Yeah!

Very cool! Earlier you said that your platform is sort of snowballing and you're growing your audience. Do you feel like you had to work for opportunities to promote your message, or do you feel that just by posting on Instagram and through word of mouth your platform grew naturally?

Well, to start with it was just a hobby, so I just posted to Instagram to sort of show off the results of what I enjoyed. And then it sort of snowballed and I started viewing it as a career possibly, with other people encouraging me to view it that way. Then I suppose I started reaching out to more newspapers and magazines, and I figured that if one wants me then maybe another one will. Then it kind of grew and over the last three years it's exploded really. I get people contacting me; a lot of autistic people contact me. WaterBear contacted me about the film, galleries contacted me, so it sort of grew quite naturally once I started viewing it as a business.

As your platform grew, what do you think was the biggest obstacle that you faced?

Definitely my social anxiety. Once the business got to a certain stage where I had to go and do gallery events or go and do speeches and things, two years ago that was really tough, so overcoming that was a big hurdle. Now I've gotten to the point where I actually enjoy going and speaking to a crowd of people, giving a presentation.

If there's a reader out there who struggles with the same thing, social anxiety in front of crowds and such, what advice would you give them for moving from being overwhelmed by anxiety to enjoying these events like you did?

The first thing I did on the first speech was pretend there wasn't an audience there - that I couldn't see them. When I looked ahead I would look at the back of the room and not at the people. Once I'd done one I just kept telling myself, 'Well, I've done one and survived, so I'll survive the next.' Then five or six down the line I started to enjoy them, speaking to people.

As you have gone to these different events as a young person, someone who is under 18, how did you stay safe? How did you prevent yourself from getting into a dangerous situation?

I knew the people who were organizing the events. I'd met those people previously, so I trusted them.

So it's just about doing your research and knowing what's happening ahead of time?

Yeah.

How would you categorize the message of your advocacy platform? What do you want the world to know, what sort of changes do you want to see in the world?

I just want people to be kinder and more accepting of each other. That's the message I use normally. To realize what a dangerous place we're in in terms of conservation. How many species are at risk. Each of us does have the power to change it.

What's the future of Alfie Bowen? What do you think your future activism will look like? Do you have any upcoming projects you want to share?

I suppose the serious thing is the book, which launches on the first of September [2021] globally, so I hope that will raise some awareness. Next year, Covid permitting, I am looking to do a UK school tour, speaking in schools and universities to raise awareness of autism and people's differences in general.

Do you have any last words of advice for a young autistic person who is aspiring to be an advocate?

Don't be afraid to share your story because there will be someone somewhere who needs to hear it.

Alfie can be found online at the following:
Instagram: @alfiebowen
On the web: www.alfiebowen.com

Kat Falacienski

Background:
Our next case study features 19-year-old Kat Falacienski from Denver, Colorado, in the USA. As a high school student, Kat rallied her classmates as a political activist for several causes, and to this day has continued to work to elevate the voices of her peers in her community. Kat is also a recipient of the Boettcher Scholarship, among the most prestigious scholarships offered to high school students in the state of Colorado.

Content warning: This case study includes references to school shootings as these tragic events relate to Kat's advocacy work. Some readers may find this content distressing. Reader discretion is advised.

So, Kat, your first experience with advocacy came when you were how old?

I was 16.

Do you want to talk a little bit about what you were feeling when you decided to get into advocacy? As I understand it, this came in the wake of the tragic Parkland, Florida, school shooting. This event caused you to organize a school walkout with a few of your friends?

Well, I had always wanted to do something about the school shootings because I thought about it all the time. Especially after Parkland, every day or every couple of days I would go to school and think like 'What if someone comes in and shoots me?' Or I would go to class, and I would think 'Where would I hide if someone came in?' Would I be able to run out the door, or would I just die, just like that? So it never really left my mind, but I was never really sure what to do until after Parkland, and then I kind of stumbled into it almost. It wasn't originally my idea, I didn't hear about the shooting and then think 'Oh I should organize a march,' it didn't occur to me until my friends started talking about it, like 'Hey, there are people thinking about organizing a march,' and then I thought 'Oh, that's such a good idea! We have to do this!'

There were other girls who were unaffiliated with us who were also thinking about this, so I kind of got all of us together and we organized a meeting with the school, and cleared it with them, and we set up a date and a time and everything. I just felt so powerful, in a way I had never felt before. It was like a high almost, like because I knew that I was doing something and that something could potentially affect thousands of other people that I didn't even know. I had never felt like that before, it was such a gratifying sort of power.

How did your walkout go down? What happened?

It was a little messy, as all protests are. But overall, it was very organized, and I would say successful in the short term. We had a huge turnout, we even had the police department there to escort us to make sure that no one would harass us or to make sure that no one ran us over with cars. They would, like, block off the streets for us, which is awesome. We had a great turnout, the turnout at East [High School] was great, also very organized. They had this whole ceremony where they read the names and short obituaries of the people who had died at Parkland, and then we all marched to the [state] capitol. We gathered around the capital and, while the protest was peaceful, we were loud and difficult to ignore.

Some legislators came out just to congratulate us. The governor, Governor [John] Hickenlooper, came out and he also congratulated us, saying, 'Oh, it's so great, you young people are so engaged, make sure to vote when you're older.' So I would say in the short term it was a success; however, in the long term it did not produce very much meaningful change.

So, as you said, this first bit of activism didn't have the impact that you wanted. Did this make you feel like you just wanted to give up, or did it encourage you to try harder? Did you feel any disappointment?

Oh, I was very disappointed, very, very disappointed. I was mad at my classmates for, you know, moving on even as more shootings continued to happen. It was basically like before, when shootings happened and we all just accepted it as normal. I was pretty depressed actually, because really we failed. I didn't know very much about activism, because neither of my parents are activists, they hadn't taught me anything, and so I didn't know what to do. It wasn't until later in the year that I learned that activism is more than just protesting; it's more than just organizing. I can write, that's what I can do, so that's what I have to do now if I want to do anything.

How did find the motivation to push forward and move on with your advocacy platform despite the disappointment? Is there anything that helped you?

The realization that I could use writing to effect change, that helped. Also, I just had to accept, and I'm still working on accepting this right now even, that it's not my responsibility to fix everything. Whenever I worry that I'm not doing enough, I have to remind myself, even now, that you can never do enough. One person can never do enough. At best, you will be a meaningfully contributing part to a larger social shift.

Do you think then that perhaps the role of an advocate is less to be the one who fixes everything themselves and more the one that inspires others to make a change in a sort of ripple effect fashion?

I would say so. I would say that the job of an activist is really just to do what they can in the circumstances that they find themselves in. Yeah, if that means inspiring others, which is kind of like the optimal outcome, that's great. If it means just taking care of yourself so you can take care of others later, that's also fine. You just have to do what you can, and you can't waste time reaching for things you know you can't do.

You said that the next avenue you took after your first intro into activism and advocacy was writing. What made you decide on writing as a medium, rather than some other avenue of communication (such as, for example, making videos)?

Well, writing was what I could do. I can't make videos very well, I don't know anything about video editing software or anything like that, I can't do door-to-door campaigning because it involves talking to a large amount of strangers, I can't do that. Writing was what I knew I could do because I've been writing my whole life. I went to school, my school was Denver School of the Arts, for writing. I auditioned for creative writing and got in, and I wrote all the time, every single day. It was what I was good at, it's still what I'm good at. There really wasn't much more to it than that, it was just like 'This is what I can do, so I might as well do it.'

We've heard now that you eventually moved on to writing for activism. Where did you write?

I wrote for *Teens Resist* and *Affinity Magazine.*

Can you tell us a little bit more about those?

Sure, so they're both teen news sites, run by and for students, which means we were unpaid because no one has any money, but that's okay. *Teens Resist,* their format, at least as it was when I was there, is that we would put out a post every month or so, and it would be just quick little summaries of news events. It was really meant for people who didn't have a lot of time on their hands or a lot of energy to follow the news, so we had to condense it down. I had my own little column where I wrote about the things that were happening in state legislatures and state assemblies that I thought were ignored too often by the mainstream media.

Affinity was much more intensive, it really functioned more like a typical news site, where we had our writers, and we were all under pressure to constantly produce new content. I think the requirement was one piece every week, but almost no one could actually do that, so often we would just have to settle for just like one piece every two weeks or one piece every three weeks because it was so difficult to keep up with one piece per week. It would take me hours and hours just to get a rough draft and get all my information there, so I imagine it took the others quite a bit of time as well.

How did you hear about the websites/magazines you were writing for? How did you get involved with them?

I read about *Teens Resist* in the magazine *Teen Vogue,* which I read regularly. I read an article in there about *Teens Resist*. It was pretty easy applying, I just had a little online application where it was like 'list your writing experience, list your activism experience,' and they got back to me within weeks and said I was good to go. With *Affinity* I literally googled 'teen news sites,' or something like that, and it was the first one to pop up and so I clicked on it, and I started reading some of the articles and they read like real news articles. I was terribly impressed, they were so well-researched, so well-written, and they had an online application as well pretty similar to *Teen's Resist,* so I applied and they let me in as well.

So you were obviously under a lot of pressure when you were working with Affinity. How did you handle that pressure? Did you ever need to give yourself a break? How did you realize when you were reaching a point where you needed to just slow down?

That's still a relatively new concept to me. When I was writing for *Teens Resist* and then for *Affinity* there was no self-care really. I just worked and worked and worked and worked until my brain was too full to do anything else and then I would kind of be forced to take 30 or 45 minutes to stim and let my brain sort of filter out everything that was happening. I was doing tons of schoolwork and tons of extra curriculars including that, and it was not sustainable.

I have autism, and so essentially I was doing so much work and taking on so much pressure that I was kind of forced to stop because my anxiety reached such levels that I was having trouble functioning. Not only did I have to seek treatment for that, which I never really had before, but I had to just admit to myself that, okay, I can't work myself to death anymore, this is unhealthy, I need to have some space to breathe, I need to stop doing so much.

Around that same time the [Covid-19] pandemic hit and we went into lockdown, which actually kind of worked out well for me in the sense that it gave me an opportunity to do nothing, because school was shut down and we had a little more slack for turning in articles and writing because every-one was dealing with the pandemic. That was part of how I learned habits of caring for myself.

So you stopped writing for these sites at some point. Do you think that came out of self-care?

It really came out of self-care, although my anxiety was so high and the news was so terrible that I literally could not read the news without feeling this intense physical pain. And you know, if you can't read the news you obviously can't write it. So yeah, my brain kind of forced me to stop.

From there, I think your next little venture into activism was when you did your letter-writing campaign, encouraging people to vote?

Yeah.

Would you like to tell us a little bit more about what you did?

So what I did was quite easy. I made an account with the web-site [Vote Forward], and they were pretty much in full swing for the 2020 elections. They had campaigns in I think at least half the states, and so you just would click on the state that you wanted and there were options like 'adopt five voters' or 'adopt 20 voters' and you just clicked on one of those but-tons and a printable list of names and addresses would pop up. You printed that out, and you printed out the templates, and then you just went through them one by one. It was like 'Dear so-and-so,' I wrote their name, 'I'm a volunteer at Vote

Forward, I'm encouraging you to vote in the 2020 election.' It was not overtly partisan, we weren't telling anyone to vote for any particular candidate, we were just telling them to vote however they wanted. There was a blank space beneath the words 'I vote because' and I essentially kind of settled into the same answer every time to make it easier because I had so many letters, and I think I wrote something like 'I'm only 18 years old, and people like me are a little afraid right now, and the future and the way to move forward and to take charge of what is happening is to vote, the best way to effect governmental change is to vote.'

I said that because I knew I was probably writing to a lot of young people because Vote Forward got their registries of voters from people who they found had not voted in the past and were unlikely to vote, which I assumed meant a lot of young people. And then I put my name on it, put it in the envelope, addressed the envelope, I put a PO box for the return address, stamped it, I decorated them, I wrote 'vote' in fancy letters, and I used glitter pens on them to make them colorful. Then we went and mailed them by the assigned deadline. I don't know how many of them reached people, or if anyone was persuaded to vote because of them. I hope so, but I did what I could, and, ultimately, it's their choice to vote.

I want to focus in on that last sentence, where you said, 'I did what I could.' This could probably be the mantra for many kinds of advocates, and I remember you talked earlier about dealing with the realization that you don't have to be the world's own personal savior. Why is advocacy meaningful, then, if you so often run into situations like you have where you're thinking, 'What I'm doing

isn't working, and nobody's listening?' Obviously, you still think
that activism is meaningful, so what have you done to keep going
and remember that what you're doing is enough?

You obviously can't expect instant results with activism. You
can't expect people to listen to you just because you're there.
I kind of I think learned this lesson not only from activism,
but also from creative writing. I would go to creative writing
classes every single day at my arts school, and we would have
a teacher tell us the real talk about being a professional writer.
It's remarkably similar I think to being an activist. The main
thing he said is, 'First of all, you're usually all alone. No one's
gonna do anything for you, you have to do things yourself,
and at the end of the day you're alone with your work. Other
people can support you, but ultimately it is an endeavor you
do yourself.' Something he said, which we all kind of vaguely
knew but he put into much more understandable phrasing,
he said that it's hard getting discovered, and it's hard to get
people to read your stuff. It's not that people are mean or cruel,
they're just busy, they have their own lives to attend to, they
have problems of their own they're trying to resolve. You can't
expect people to listen to you just because you both happen
to be in the same space.

I already knew that if I was going to pursue writing it
was going to be difficult to get anyone to listen to what I
had to say, and so I sort of applied that to activism as well.
You do what you can because it is better than doing nothing,
and because maybe at some point in the future someone
will listen to what you have to say, because really you don't
know who's going to read your work. Say, after you're dead

for example, you don't know the life your work is going to take on. And, second, this applies more to activism than to writing, movements are made up of people. Movements are made up of individuals who all happen to be working together. Thus, the movement rests on every individual. If you can be an individual in a movement, you are contributing. You are contributing to something that may change history. It doesn't mean you're doing it all yourself, but you're doing something.

What have been your biggest recurring challenges as an advocate?

I would say that my biggest recurring challenge has just been putting myself out there, and that's really more a me problem than an advocacy problem. I'm just so afraid of people, I really am. I'm afraid of people, and so it's hard to be around what you're afraid of all the time. That's why a lot of my activism work ended up being remote - that way I didn't have to talk to people directly. So I would say that has been my biggest challenge, but I'm thankful that now in the age of the internet there are a lot of ways to get around having to talk to people directly.

Imagine that there is a teen or young adult autistic person stand-ing in front of you who wants to be an advocate. What advice do you give them?

Well first of all, I'd tell them a lot of the same things I've told you before: you don't have to do everything, you don't have to be a star or anything like that, you don't have to be on the news even, you just have to do what you can in the circumstances that you find yourself in. And those circumstances are going to change - maybe some days you are receiving a lot of accommodations or have a lot of support and you are able to do more than other days. Maybe some days you don't do anything at all. I have days where I can't do anything at all, and that is okay. You do not have to work yourself to death. You might have to do things that you're uncomfortable with, but don't do things you wouldn't ordinarily do, especially not to please other people or other activists. You do what you know that you can do safely.

I would also say that you're probably going to catch flack from people, maybe not like the news, but maybe your parents or your friends or your family for being autistic and putting yourself out there, especially if you're advocating for other autistic people. It's hard; it's really hard. This goes back to what I was saying about how sometimes you're all alone with it, and your only motivation for keeping yourself going has to come from within you. You can't rely on other people to validate you, or tell you that you're doing a good job, or keep you going; you have to keep yourself going.

Kat can be found online at the following:
On the web, via *Affinity Magazine*: www.affinitymagazine.us/author/kat-falacienski

Emily Katy

Background:
Our final case study will cover 20-year-old autism and

mental health advocate Emily Katy from the United Kingdom. After struggling with anxiety and being diagnosed with autism as a teenager, Emily began blogging and sharing her experiences through Twitter. Emily is also an NHS governor and a trustee for the Autistic Girls Network.

Content warning: This case study includes references to self-harm and attempted suicide as they relate to Emily's experiences with mental illness. Some readers may find this content distressing. Reader discretion is advised.

So you have had plenty of your own experiences when it comes to struggling with mental health. If you don't mind sharing, what are the earliest struggles you remember having with mental health?

As a child I was always quite anxious, but I hid it very well. I think I learned that I didn't want to stand out, basically. When I was 13 my grandfather died, and I think that just triggered a whole bunch of stuff. I started having panic attacks every day, which then kind of morphed into OCD. My OCD started off kind of being like 'Hey, look, I can help you kind of control your anxiety.' It was like 'if you do this then that won't happen. If you tap that a certain amount of times then your mum won't die,' so it was kind of a way for me to control my anxiety, but then the OCD got out of control as well. I think with all the anxiety and the OCD I kind of started feeling very low. I started self-harming. I then got to a place where I just didn't really want to live anymore. I suppose this all happened over about three years I'd say, my panic attacks started when I was about 13 and when I was 16 I ended up in hospital, so over those few years the OCD got worse and my depression kind of kicked in.

You've mentioned before that you spent some time in the hospital because of your mental health. When you were admitted to the hospital and sectioned, meaning you couldn't leave, would you say that was your lowest point?

To some extent, but I think that over the next couple of years I reached lower points that I didn't think I could reach. Interestingly, when I was first admitted to the hospital I had agreed to go, and then once I was there I asked to leave and that's when they sectioned me, and that's when I couldn't leave. I actually think I reached lower points after that once I was out of hospital for the first time.

So you've reached your lowest point. What caused you to start building your way back up? What was the upswing like after that?

For a couple of years, say from when I was 16 until I was 18, I was kind of in and out of hospital, I attempted to take my life a few times. I got to the summer, and I wanted to go to uni at first to study psychology, but I ended up changing my mind and I wanted to go and study mental health nursing. I basically realized that I had to sort myself out if I wanted to be a mental health nurse, and at the same time my advocacy stuff online started. I initially literally just started tweeting about autism and it just grew from there.

What made you want to start tweeting about autism?

I don't really know, I just got on Twitter one day and I just... I don't know, I don't really remember what I first tweeted about, I think it might have been like World Autism Awareness Day or something, and I just put out a tweet and I was kind of amazed by the response that I go to it, and I was like, 'Oh wow, people care!' Or at least that's what I thought at first.

Because I was getting a response online, I was like, 'Oh, if I keep doing this I'll get to connect with other autistic people,' and I think that's really what made me keep going with it - that I suddenly found this whole community of autistic people online that I never knew existed. The amount I learned from them, I learned so much, like so quickly to some extent but at the same time I feel like I still learn a lot every day from other autistic people's experiences.

I really connect with that, because I had the exact same experience, where I sort of figured out there is this rich autistic community online. Would you say that finding people who are like you or who you can relate to was a big confidence booster for you?

Definitely, because I didn't really know any autistic people. It's funny because now I know quite a few autistic people and funnily enough a lot of them I met in hospital and along my journey in the mental health system who were then late diagnosed, with a lot of them being diagnosed after me. At the time I didn't know any other autistic people in my real life, and I also felt very torn over the fact that I still had a very ableist and very bad understanding of autism, just from what I knew and what I had grown up with, from what everyone says every day. People would say to me, 'How can you have been diagnosed with autism?' I think I had that so much in my head that when I found this online autistic community, where people were having the same exact problems as I was having, people were being challenged over their diagnosis, people were expressing about how this kind of autism stereotype is true for some but isn't true for others. I learned that I didn't have to look autistic to be autistic, and I think that was just a massive revelation.

I believe that at this point you were already blogging about your experiences as well. Your current website, Authentically Emily, was that your first website?

No, it wasn't. I actually started blogging when I was about 13, initially about like anxiety and stuff that has nothing to do with autism. Well, I don't know, I suppose it was an undiagnosed autistic's perspective! Authentically Emily is my new thing, I actually only started it earlier this year [2021].

Going all the way back to when you were 13, what made you decide to start writing about mental health?

I actually remember different teachers suggesting it to me, saying that I have a lot of opinions, so they were like, 'It would probably be good for you to get your words out on paper.' I always loved writing as a child, so it was actually suggested to me. I started blogging anonymously, and I would kind of just blog about how my day was, blog about how I was feeling.

It wasn't very educational or informative, it was a bit like a diary that I put online. People would see it and respond, and it felt quite comforting, like I had a little bit of an outlet.

Do you think that for you writing in a diary format was helpful for processing your emotions and thoughts?

Yeah, I think at the time that was what I needed. It wasn't just me blogging, I also read other people's blogs and at the time I was just kind of connecting with people who had anxiety, because that's what I thought I had.

After you came out of the hospital for mental illness, you got involved with your local CAMHS council and eventually were elected to be a governor for your local NHS trust. How did you get involved with these opportunities?

When I came out of hospital, I basically joined my local CAMHS young people's council, which looks at improving the CAMHS services in our area, including the hospital that I was in. It gave us a bit of an advisory role, as well as feeling like we were giving something back and making a bit of a difference. Through that, one of the governors from the NHS trust that we were under came and asked if anyone would like to stand for election because they were basically like a young person's voice on the council of governors, and so I was very enthusiastic and I was like, 'Yeah, sure, I'll stand for election!'

I was elected, and that role as a governor for my local NHS trust basically involves me holding the people in charge of the trust accountable for their actions, making sure they're meeting targets, reviewing important decisions that are made such as who's in leadership roles, accepting who's in different positions, and things like that. I just finished my first three-year term of that, and I was recently re-elected, so I'm going into my second three-year term as a governor.

What do you think was the greatest benefit that you got out of being on the youth council?

I was a 16-year-old with a lot of inbuilt anger at the world and at everything I had gone through, and I think that I needed an outlet to express that healthily. Joining the CAMHS youth council gave me an outlet to express my experience and express what I felt could have been done better, and express what I thought was going well, and kind of get involved with shaping the service, and I think that benefited me massively.

As a CAMHS youth representative and as an NHS governor, do you feel like you actually saw some real change take place from the work you were doing on those boards?

At times I did; to be fair I did feel listened to by a lot of the people in charge. A lot of them gave me a lot of time and also did kind of take into account the problems that there were in the services and did seek to improve that. We did see different things come into place: we developed a new website for the trust, there are no procedures in place for different services that we were a part of forming, so yes there was some change during my time there.

By the way you approached that question, I sort of get the feeling that it didn't always go 100 percent how you would have wanted?

I think that change is slow, funding is limited, and priorities are often set nationally as well as locally, so we often have to follow the national strategies. I think there's a lot more we could do if we had unlimited funding, unlimited time, and unlimited passionate people.

Was it ever frustrating having to work within the confines of what funding and priorities allowed you to do rather than trying to fulfil a grand vision you may have had?

I think you get a bunch of very enthusiastic teenagers on a CAMHS board, and they have unlimited visions of the future that when it comes down to it are not always practically possible. Things take time, unfortunately change is slow, and, yeah, it's been frustrating, but then I also get to be part of looking at what can be done, and that's really powerful too.

While you were working as an NHS governor, were you also continuing to use Twitter like you had been previously doing?

Yeah, but in that time I think it grew massively. My Twitter usage has expanded over the past few years. It started with me just kind of tweeting odd stuff, which was I suppose at the start of my governor role, to me now using it quite a lot. During that time as a governor I was tweeting, learning a lot from autistic people, reading a lot of autistic people's blogs. I was reading up on the history of autism, reading a lot about autism politics, learning just so much. That was when I started writing my own stuff. I had a couple of articles published by different places during that time and I gave a couple of talks at different places on my experience.

How did you grow your Twitter audience?

That is a good question, and I wish I knew the answer. I honestly don't know. I just started tweeting and I started connecting with people. I don't know why people started following me to be honest. People just did, and it slowly grew.

You've talked about how finding the autistic community and connecting with other autistic people has been very positive for you. What do you think is the greatest benefit that you have gotten from connecting with other autistic people online?

A sense of understanding, of inclusion, that you don't get, or I certainly don't get, as an autistic person in everyday life. You click on an app, you open the app, and suddenly you're surrounded by people who understand you, people who are non-judgmental. I suddenly felt connected with people who understood, and it just really helped me to understand myself better. Also, to learn about other people I suddenly became so invested in understanding different people's experiences and understanding why some people are thriving and others are not.

Did you stay primarily on Twitter, or did you use other social media platforms? What drew you to primarily use Twitter?

I stayed mainly on Twitter. I have an Instagram account that I do not use very often, and I do not have much of a following on. I just don't find [Instagram] as engaging as Twitter, or as connecting, if you know what I mean.

So, at this point you're growing your presence on Twitter to the point that people are noticing you're writing articles in various places. Why did you decide to write articles over some other method of communicating your message?

I think it was just what was available to me. I like writing, I find writing quite therapeutic. It comes quite naturally to me, writing, and it always has. I think that I like writing as a way of expressing myself a lot more than I like talking. I find writing to be an easy way to express myself. When people have given me the opportunities to write for them, providing I agree with what their organization believes, I have been very grateful to be able to use that platform.

At this point in your career as an advocate, you're growing a following on Twitter, you have responsibilities with the NHS, and you're doing your fair share of writing and public speaking. The internet, especially when you start to get a following and people start reaching out to you, can become a little bit dangerous. How did you keep yourself safe?

That's a good question. I guess by not giving out super personal information. I know that the nature of advocacy is sharing quite personal information, but it's not sharing my address, or I try not to share my full name. It's not sharing information that could put me physically at risk. In terms of protecting my mental health from it all, there's a great button called 'report' and a great button called 'block,' which I have harnessed many times. I don't check my private DMs very often, because I get a lot of inappropriate photographs in my DMs, which isn't very nice.

Yeah, I think that's just the danger of being a young person online, specifically probably a young woman online. I don't know, young boys maybe get similar but slightly different dangerous things, but yeah.

Earlier this year [2021], you got involved with the Autistic Girls Network. How did that come about?

I was contacted by Cathy Wassell, the now-CEO of the Autistic Girls Network, and basically she just approached me on Twitter and was like, 'Hey, do you want to be involved, do you want to be a trustee for us?' Autistic Girls Network does not quite have charity status yet, but we're working on it. Originally it was a Facebook group where mainly parents of autistic girls kind of came to share their difficulties in getting diagnosed, the challenges they were facing, and it kind of expanded beyond that. Cathy had a vision for it, she wanted it to be an actual charity, she wanted it to be an actual organization that could help autistic girls and their families. She's taken it to more platforms than just Facebook, obviously she's taken it to Twitter, and we now have a trustee board. We have an elected CEO, we've sorted out the bank statusing and stuff like that. We are currently waiting to be approved as a charity.

As you mentioned earlier, you've recently launched your new blog Authentically Emily. What made you decide to start a new website rather than stick with the one you had been using for so many years previously?

I wanted to create a place that has resources on it, and not just resources but also gives my experience on different things based on the feedback I've had from autistic people, specifically autistic girls and parents of autistic people, about some of the stuff I write about. It's quite phenomenal really. When I write a blog post I still find it quite difficult to think that it can help people, because it's a blog post that I've just sat in my room and written, but apparently it makes a difference for people. I wanted a fresh website that I could publish all my stuff on rather than just scrolling through my Twitter, which I think is kind of lengthy and where resources disappear, whereas on a website everything is easy to access.

And then there's the Not Alone Talk that you've been hosting. Would you like to tell us about it?

Not Alone Talk was an hourly chat that was started by someone called April on Twitter last year during [Covid-19] lockdown, and since then it's been used every day as a space where people can come and just talk about random stuff and ask silly questions. The reason it was started was to help combat loneliness during coronavirus, and we now have quite a lot of regulars who log on every night, and it's a nice community space that people can come to and just kind of connect with each other. I got involved with that last year, and I host it once a week now, which is fun.

If there's a theme that seems to keep coming up throughout your journey as an advocate, it's probably community. What is the value of community to you? How has bringing people together helped you as an advocate?

I think that as an autistic person I grew up feeling very misunderstood and very disconnected from people and from the world. I felt very confused, and even though I had friends I felt very alone because I felt so different. I think that being able to build or being part of a community in an online space is very powerful, especially for those who have felt or still feel very disconnected in their life. It provides a space of inclusion for people who don't always feel included, or at least it aims to provide that, because I know there are still things we need to do better and there are still people who feel like they don't belong in these places. For example, I know a lot of Black autistic people who feel like they have been pushed out of the autistic community, and these are things that we need to look at and focus on as well when we talk about feeling connected in these spaces.

Do you think it's important then for us to consider the people who are not just like ourselves when we take actions as activists?

Yeah, it's definitely important for us to listen to and raise the voices of those who aren't necessarily always accepted and understood. I'm thinking specifically about multiply margin-alized people. It's so important that we listen to them as well and raise their voices and remember that when we're talking about being accepted we might feel accepted, but that doesn't mean that everyone does.

Do you think that it's possible that even if you have the best of intentions and are trying to do the right thing you might acciden-tally hurt somebody else?

Oh, for sure! Yes, there is definitely that possibility and it happens every day! People can be harmed even when we don't mean to, but that doesn't mean that we don't have to take that responsibility and look at ourselves and see what we're doing wrong and see how we can fix that. Just because we don't intend to hurt someone doesn't mean it isn't our responsibility to fix that.

For almost your whole life it sounds like you've struggled with mental health. Since becoming an advocate, how have you continued to manage your mental health to prevent yourself from falling into another crisis like you have been in many times before?

First, being able to understand how being autistic impacts my mental health has been absolutely massive because I wasn't able to regulate my mental health without understanding that I was autistic and without understanding that certain things tipped me over the edge in a way that they didn't for other people. Over the last few years I have learned a lot more about being autistic and how that impacts my mental health, and being aware of that has meant that I can put strategies in place to mitigate those things. Additionally, I've worked very hard with my mental health team, which I've been very privileged to access, and they've really helped me navigate stuff. Yeah, so therapy.

Let's see, what else has helped? Just kind of the support from my friends, my family, as they have grown to understand me more has really helped.

What do you see as being next for your work as an advocate?

It still seems funny to me sometimes that I have this advocacy platform, I still kind of see myself as just kind of opening up Twitter or opening up my laptop and just kind of typing my experience, and for people to read that and connect with that still baffles me. I don't feel like I have this sort of position as an advocate. But I guess I do. I'm privileged enough to have this following so I will continue using it. I will continue amplifying other people's voices, continue writing about my own stuff, continue being an NHS governor, and I'm very excited for the future of Autistic Girls Network and the great stuff we're going to be able to do through that. I don't really know what the future holds, I guess I just sort of keep rolling on day by day and seeing where life takes me.

What last little pieces of advice would you give to a young autistic person who wants to be an advocate?

I say to always listen to other autistic people as well. Take on board other people's perspectives and amplify other people's voices as well as your own. In getting started as an advocate, I would say to honestly just be true to yourself, portray who you are as a person, and be honest and authentic.

Emily can be found online at the following:
Twitter: @ItsEmilyKaty
Instagram: @itsemilykaty
On the web: www.authenticallyemily.uk

Parting Words

So here we are, at the end of the book. You've made it through, and now all that is left for you to do is to put yourself out there and start bringing your vision of positive change to the world. By deciding to be an advocate, you are hiking down a trail that you are blazing yourself, towards an end point that is simultaneously in sight and an unknowable distance away. But one thing is for sure: the trail will be long and uneven, but also highly rewarding, and it will teach you things about yourself that you never thought you would get to know. As an autistic young person, you are in a perfect position to hike this trail, and it is highly commendable to decide to take action not because it is the easy thing to do, not because it is the most glamorous thing to do, but because it is the right thing to do. As young people, we are in a position right now to dictate what our future will look like. And as autistic people, our unique neurological makeup makes us the perfect people to become activists for change, if only we are supported properly.

Advocacy truly is a mindset, and one that I hope you can use to resolve the problems that you burn to see resolved. I hope you can use it to promote a better future for yourself and others. I hope that you will commit to being an everyday advocate: using the things you have learned here to bring about change within your community simply through the actions that you take each day.

I hope that this guide has been useful to you, and I hope that you can continue to use it as a reference as you travel further down your trail towards change. I hope that having a resource such as this to help you advocate specifically as an autistic person has helped to illuminate an otherwise dark path. I hope that the stories and insights of all the advocates who were presented in this book have given you guidance, inspiration, and a set of role models to look up to. Nothing would make me happier than if you used the information written here to make a real difference in the world. But, ultimately, I have done my job if you simply walk away from this book in a better place than where you were when you started.

It was a pleasure writing for you. I bid you farewell and good luck. I believe in you.

You got this.